THE POCKET BOOK OF THE

Corvette

ANDREW MONTGOMERY

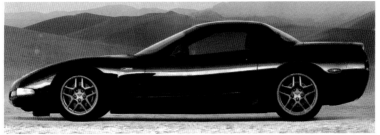

T H E   P O C K E T   B O O K   O F   T H E

Corvette

The Definitive Guide to the All American Sports Car

SALAMANDER

To Bill and Og

Published by Salamander Books Ltd.
8 Blenheim Court
Brewery Road
London N7 9NT

© Salamander Books Ltd., 2003

A member of **Chrysalis** Books plc

9 8 7 6 5 4 3 2 1

ISBN 1 84065 517 8

All correspondence concerning the content of this volume should be addressed to Salamander Books Ltd.

Credits
Commissioning Editor: Marie Clayton
Design and Layout: Hardlines Ltd, Charlbury, Oxford
Picture Research: Andrew Montgomery
Reproduction: Anorax
Printed in China

Picture Credits
All pictures Copyright © Chrysalis Images except for the following:

James Mann
166, 170-1, 172-3, 202-3, 204-5, 206-7, 214, 220-1, 222-3, 224-5, 232-3, 234-5, 236-7, 245-6, 248-9, 253, 254-5, 259-60, 284-5, 291-2, 294, 296-7, 298-9, 300-1, 324, 360-1, 383, 386, 384, 385, 387, 389, 390-1, 392, 394-5, 396, 399, 401, 402, 405, 406, 409, 411, 412, 414-5, 416-7, 418-9, 422, 425, 427, 428-9, 430-1, 433, 434-5, 437, 438-9, 440-1, 442-3, 445, 446, 447-8

By kind permission of Chevrolet Corvette Division of general Motors
3, 5 bottom right, 8, 9, 450, 451, 452-3, 454-5

Contents

Introduction

sports car
n (1928): a low small usu. 2 passenger automobile designed for quick response, easy maneuverability, and high-speed driving.

That's what it is, according to Merriam Webster's Collegiate Dictionary. The date that the term first appeared—1928—indicates that it is most probably European in origin. In 1928, super-charged Bentleys and Mercedes-Benz were racing at Brooklands and LeMans, along with Bugattis and Alfa Romeos. Sports cars were being produced in every country in Europe whilst in the United States, Errett Lobban Cord was just about to unveil the superb, front-wheel-drive L-29 to fill the gap between his attractive and attractively priced Auburns, and his magnificent and monumentally expensive Duesenbergs. The legendary Stutz Blackhawk was ready to go into production; the stage was set for America to take on the world with home-produced performance cars that would equal and surpass anything built in Britain, Italy, France or Germany—but the Great Depression intervened. In the lean and hungry years of the nineteen-thirties, many of the greatest names in the American Automobile industry passed into history and folklore, Cord, Auburn, Duesenberg and Stutz among them. The Stock Market collapse of '29 put paid to the idea of a true sports car being designed and built in the United States for a generation, but the babies born into the tumult that followed the Wall Street Crash would, by the time they reached their twenties, be able to enjoy a period of unparalleled American prosperity while much of Europe was reduced to rubble and its people were still reeling from the horrors of the Second World War.

It was in 1927, a year before the term "sports car" was first coined, that the man who, more than any other, was responsible for giving America her very own sports car, joined the General Motors Corporation. During his long reign as Head of GM's styling studio—originally called the Art and Colour Section—Harley Earl oversaw the design of over fifty million vehicles. Many of these have achieved iconic status: the

Left: Chevrolet Corvette, 1953: truck motor, bus tires and 2-speed transmisson; one of the greatest automotive stories ever told starts here.

Below: You've come a long way, baby. The latest generation of Corvettes are amongst the most technologically advanced automobiles in the world, but they remain true to their proud and unique heritage.

Far right: One of the most enviable positions in motoring: the driving seat of a Corvette.

1927 LaSalle, the Buick Roadmaster, the Cadillac Eldorado and the Tri-Chevys. "Misterearl", often derided for his bullying behavior and his fondness for fins and chrome, may well be judged by history to have been the most influential designer of the twentieth century. Earl's bold, innovative, uncompromising, All-American approach to automobile styling can be summed up in one car—in one word: Corvette.

For half a century the Corvette has been acknowledged to be America's first and foremost performance car—the original and best. The Corvette may justly be described as the flagship of the mighty General Motors Corporation, the largest producer of automobiles in the world. During its fifty years of continuous production, this car has embodied the changing tastes of the American motorist but has remained, at all times, an object of

desire to which millions aspire. Despite its shaky first steps, the Corvette has consistently managed to out-perform the most glamorous offerings of companies like Aston Martin, Porsche and Ferrari. Even after the considerable price increases of the latest, super-sophisticated generation, the 'Vette still offers a lot more bangs per buck than the products of Newport Pagnell, Stuttgart or Maranello. The adherence of the Corvette's engineers and designers down the years to the sound, simple, robust and reliable basic principles preferred by American drivers has produced a car that can deliver gut-wrenching performance without stomach-turning running costs or constant maintenance headaches. Owning and driving a Corvette is, for an American, at once a patriotic statement and a demonstration of good sense.

1953–1955
The Grand Original

Below: The inspiration for the styling of the first generation Corvettes was an unlikely mixture of traditional English sports cars like the MG TD and Harley Earl's love affair with airplane design.

In the Beginning

In the austere years immediately following the end of the Second World War, everybody was ready for some fun, and none more than the British, who would continue to endure rationing until well into the 'fifties. American servicemen based in England were able to sample one of the earliest manifestations of post-war jollification in the shape of the MG sports car. William Richard Morris, later to become Lord Nuffield, was the Henry Ford of

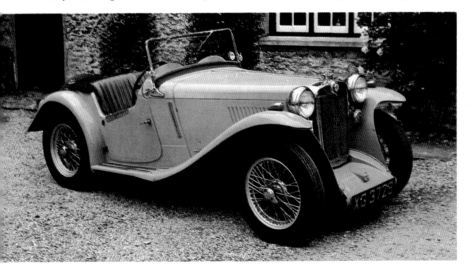

the British automobile industry. Morris Garages had produced their first sports car in 1923 and the post-war TC was in the classic mold: crude and cramped, with a simple, ladder-frame chassis and a tiny, 1,250 cc motor, but it was a whole lot of fun for a guy to drive and the kind of car that girls liked to be driven in. It was about youth and fun and fresh air, and America took it to her heart. Other British sports cars soon started to follow the MG across the pond, bringing a whole new way of motoring to a generation raised on Detroit's diet of sedate sedans. Ninety per cent of the 1949 production run of the Jaguar XK 120 found homes in America, along with the majority of Triumph TR's and Austin-Healeys. A few US auto makers attempted to get in on the act but with little success: the Nash-Healey and the Crosley Super Sport were short lived, as was the attractive

Below: Detachable side-screens a la MG plus tail lamps courtesy of Lockheed. Result: an elegant, unified, instantly recognizable design.

Left: Harley Earl:
Misterearl gave the
world the fin, the
wrap-around
windshield, and the
two-tone paint job.
He was the King of
Chrome and the
father of the
Corvette.

Kaiser-Darrin, but the Kaiser had something that pointed the
way to the future: that curvaceous body, with its unique – and
wholly impractical – sliding doors, was made up of panels
molded in Glass Reinforced Plastic.

Harley Earl had been producing "Dream Cars"—or at least
dream designs—since the Buick Y-Job of 1937 and in 1951 came
up with the amazing Buick Le Sabre. The Le Sabre incorporated
a number of styling details deeply beloved of Misterearl, gleaned
from aerospace design in general and the Lockheed P38—known
in Europe as the Lightning – in particular. Designed to a 1937 US
Army Air Corps specification, the P38 used twin, Allison
V-1710–27 (29) 1,115 HP, liquid cooled engines. Allison was a
division of General Motors, and so it was that Earl, along with
some of his team, got the chance to go and view the prototype at
Selfridge Air Force Base, just outside of Detroit. The party was
not permitted to go closer than thirty feet but even at that range,
Earl was able to take in details that would characterize his work,
and thereby the look of the American automobile, for the next
quarter of a century and beyond. The P38 had a bubble cockpit,
a bullet-shaped nose and tapering, twin tail booms that ended in
elegant fins. The dye was cast.

The stars that would portend the birth of the Corvette were
slowly coming into alignment. In 1949, at GM's fabulous,
annual, travelling auto-circus. *Motorama*, the brain-child of the
Corporation's president and wonder-salesman, Harlow "Red"
Curtice, Earl and his merry band showed the public what they
were planning, to gauge their reaction. Generally, it was hugely
favorable. In '51, the Le Sabre caused a sensation. The
influences of the P38 were there for all to see: a massive, fake,
air intake in the nose and flowing, fish-tail fins. The Le Sabre
was fabulous, but it wasn't a sports car, it was a massive,
luxury cruiser: the proto-Eldo. By early 1952, encouraged by

many of the fertile minds around him, including the young Robert F. McLean, a great sports car lover, fresh from the California Institute of Technology, with degrees in both engineering and industrial design, Earl had made his mind up to build something light and quick-handling that would wipe the floor with anything that the Limeys could produce.

Chevrolet's sales had halved, from two million to little over one, between 1948 and 1952. Their model range was stodgy and conservative and really not worthy of the proud name that they carried. The great racer, Louis Chevrolet, who founded the company in 1911, in partnership with William Durant, the founder of General Motors, would have been deeply saddened to see the wallowing tide that rolled off the production line by the early 'fifties. The trouble was that Earl and his co-conspirators had to convince not only Curtice that the thing would sell, but also Thomas H. Keating, Chevrolet's General Manager, who was an arch-conservative. Despite the fact that sales of (predominantly British) sports cars had increased proportionately to Chevrolet's nearly doubling, from 6000 to over 11,000 in 1952, they still represented a microscopic portion of the total auto market—one car in every four thousand sold! Part of Earl's pitch would be that the car could be produced cheaply, using mostly stock Chevrolet mechanics, but that it would be striking enough to draw people into the showrooms, where maybe somebody might be able to sell them an offering from the "standard" range.

Just as the plans for the new car were being hatched, a Californian boat builder by the name of Bill Tritt caused a minor stir with a GRP bodied sports car based on a Jeep chassis. Called the Alembic I, the car was rolled into the viewing auditorium at GM's styling studio for evaluation. Earl realized that forming the body for his proposed sports car out of GRP would be far cheaper than having to produce original dies to stamp out steel body panels. GRP could be molded into the complex, curvaceous shapes that Earl loved, it was incredibly strong, light—and it didn't rust. Most important: the employment of GRP would make it possible to recover the cost of tooling up for a new vehicle with a far smaller production run than would be feasible for one of Chevrolet's standard offerings.

In the first months of 1952, Earl began work with Ed Cole, a brilliant engineer who had transferred from Cadillac in 1951 and became chief engineer the following year. Two experimental

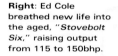

Right: Ed Cole breathed new life into the aged, "*Stovebolt Six*," raising output from 115 to 150bhp.

vehicles were built. The first, a Chevrolet convertible, suffered a massive crash at GM's Milford proving ground. The positive outcome of this unfortunate accident was that it demonstrated, more eloquently that any scientific paper, the remarkable resilience of the GRP bodywork. The second car was a small, open, two-seater sports car, codename Project Opel. By employing as many stock components as possible it was planned that the car could be sold for around $2,000, about the same as the average family sedan, and a lot cheaper than an MG or a Jaguar.

The first viewing of Project Opel (in plaster model form) was in April '52. Curtice and Keating were both present and the

Below: Harley Earl himself owned a curvaceous and elegant Jaguar XK120 and its lines undoubtedly influenced early Corvette styling.

decision was unanimous and favorable. Maybe it was thought that such a daring move would serve to revitalize Chevrolet's dowdy image and depressing sales. Whatever the reasoning behind it was, the order was given to produce a practical prototype in time for the next *Motorama*. The engineers were shown the model in June and informed that the car was to be running by January.

The resultant design had exactly the same wheelbase as the Jaguar XK120—102 ins. Young mister McLean decided to ignore convention and design the chassis from the back to the front, starting with the line of the back axle and then locating the passenger compartment, the front bulkhead and the front axle as close to the ground as possible in order to achieve the low-slung, ground-hugging profile that Earl desired. The driver and passenger would sit pretty much on the floor, rather than on the sofa. The roofline was a very low—for the period—47 inches. The low, squat feel of the car was further enhanced by wide front and rear track: 57 and 59 inches respectively. Not only did this package enable the car to look good, it also provided the basis for good handling. The motor would be placed 3 inches closer to the ground than on any previous Chevrolet model, setting the center of gravity low. It was also set much farther back than was common practice, being a full 7 inches closer to the passenger compartment bulkhead. This provided near-perfect weight distribution: not quite 50/50, but close enough, at a time when a lot of American cars carried their motors almost over the front axle, at 53/47 front to rear.

McLean's decision to adopt a chassis with box-section side-members, stiffened with a solid cross-member, meant that it would be impossible to adapt an existing chassis. The rear suspension incorporated a Hotchkiss drive system instead of

Above & Right: The venerable "Stovebolt Six" was a Chevrolet truck motor dating from 1927, hardly sporting but effectively indestructible. Ed Cole's boys managed to raise horsepower from 115bhp to 150, allowing a three figure top speed.

Chevy's standard Torque-Tube. The leaf springs were located outboard of the chassis members in an attempt to improve high speed stability. The cost of all this made it imperative that the maximum number of existing parts be used elsewhere in the design in order to keep the costs within the brief. Front suspension was therefore provided by standard parallel wishbones and coils from a Chevrolet saloon, up-rated and given an anti-roll bar. The drum brakes were standard-issue Chevy, with the master cylinders enlarged to give the pedal more feel. Steering was via a recirculating ball system from GM-Saginaw. The transmission, which would come in for much adverse comment, was Chevrolet's tried and trusted, two-speed Powerglide unit.

Ed Cole's search for a motor worthy of a true sports car was pretty fruitless. The only engine that would fit the chassis, if not the bill, was a pre-war unit intended for use in trucks, the 235 cu.in. "Stovebolt" straight-six. This unit was extremely tough and reliable but was designed to be low-revving, which was hardly what was required. Ed Cole managed to increase output from 115bhp at 3600rpm to 150bhp at 4500rpm. Torque climbed from 204lb. ft. at 2000rpm to 223lb. ft. at 2400rpm. This was achieved by the introduction of a high-lift, long-dwell camshaft, utilizing mechanical tappets in place of the hydraulic originals, along with dual-rate valve springs. An aluminum dual-intake manifold was adopted, the cylinder head was subtly modified and the compression ration raised from 7.5:1 to 8.0:1. The cooling system was improved and a triple set of Carter YH carburetors was fitted, using side-drafts in order to fit below the low hood line. The big, four-blade fan was accommodated by lowering the water pump; even the front of the rocker cover had to be shaved off to fit. Theoretically, the car was capable of around 110mph.

Opposite: The '53 Corvette's styling details were unique and instantly recognizable. The wire stone guards were later deleted as they contravened regulations in some states are were considered too "feminine."

Below: Whatever the origins of its styling, the Corvette looked, as it still does, like an All-American automobile.

The interior was given a faintly European flavor, drawing on the Jaguar XK 120 for inspiration: bucket seats and a central instrument binnacle. The exterior was totally original and distinctive. The car looked long and low, its slab sides relieved by chrome rubbing strips. The headlights were faired in to the bodywork and equipped with integral, wire stone-guards, whilst the rear lights, in a flash of aeronautical inspiration, were set in embryonic fins that had fins of their own. Bumpers were relegated to the status of ornament, consisting of delicate, chrome units fixed to the fenders. The wrap-around windshield echoed fighter plane design as well, and the radiator grille, with its thirteen, gleaming, chromium teeth, was unquestionably

aggressive. The car had a suitably masculine, muscular, almost predatory look. It was a stunner, and the decision was made to go into production. The car was to be named after a small, fast, maneuverable warship that had distinguished itself in the Second World War: The Corvette was born.

Left & Previous Page: Full of youth, vigor, freedom and confidence, the 1953 Corvette is a symbolic summation of post-war America.

Previous Page: The hood was not the original Corvette's strong point, either in terms of style or of practicality.

Right: The crossed-flag motif has graced the Corvette for half a century and remains as desirable a badge as any.

Opposite: Panel fit was a problem on early cars, as was the fitting of the awkward, canvas side-screens.

The eager crowds who swarmed into the grand ballroom of New York's Waldorf Astoria Hotel in January 1953 were completely bowled over at the sight of Chevrolet's amazing offering. The Corvette, finished in Polo White with a bright red interior, was displayed on a revolving turntable against a silvered photograph of the Manhattan skyline. As the great *Motorama* caravan traveled on, via Chicago, Dallas, Kansas City, Miami, Los Angeles and San Francisco, over four million people came to gaze—but how many of them would buy?

Keen to capitalize on the incredible success of the Corvette's *Motorama* debut, General Motors management decreed that production should commence in June 1953. This was exactly a year after chassis and engine work had begun and a mere six months after the first model had been unveiled as a "design exercise." Despite the apparent impossibility of the deadline, the first production Corvette rolled off the line at Flint, Michigan, on June 30, 1953, but right from the start, the Corvette suffered from a what might be termed a conflict of interest. The term sports car was generally accepted as indicating that a car had race-track performance, along with the noise and discomfort that that usually entailed. In order to make the new model appealing to the wider American public, who were used to being cocooned and cosseted rather than getting shaken, rattled and rolled the Corvette offered "comfort and convenience" causing it to fall woefully short of the expectations of many sports car enthusiasts, whilst its sporting pretensions alienated it from those who regarded it as an attractive, boulevard cruiser. In this regard, the crude, clip-on side curtains with Plexi-glass windows were a major turn-off. Not only was this arrangement drafty and prone to leaks, it had to be penetrated, when the hood was erected, in order to get into the car, as there were no exterior door handles. This was not the kind of thing to create a favorable impression on the kind of girls that a 1953 Corvette buyer might reasonably be expecting to impress.

Left: The epitome of elegance... The line of the '54 Motorama hard-top was a great improvement on the canvas hood but it wasn't offered until 1956, on a radically revised Corvette.

The two-speed transmission was hardly likely to appeal to those who craved the seat-of-the-pants driving experience of an MG and the engine lacked punch. Tuning the triple carburetors was a delicate task and would result in either smooth idling or crisp throttle response, but not both, similarly they could be adjusted to allow the motor to run sweetly in either hot or cold temperatures, but not both. The

Right: For all it's much-publicised shortcomings, the '53 Corvette remains a handsome and purposeful-looking car.

Below: The rear aspect is as clean cut and uncluttered as the front, though the exhaust tended to stain the pure white bodywork.

brakes still lacked feel and were alarmingly prone to fade, whilst the handling was rather less than taut.

To cap it all, or rather to end it all, it was discovered that, by some strange, aerodynamic twist of fate, exhaust gases were sucked back in the slipstream to stain the white bodywork. For a while consideration was given to forming the Corvette's bodywork out of alloy but the cost factor weighed in favor of sticking with GRP.

The final sticker price was $3490, $1000 more than an MG and a little under $1000 less than the Jaguar XK120, which was considered distinctly up-market. The success of the Corvette's introduction at *Motorama* encouraged the belief that as many as 20,000 cars might be sold annually, but it was decided, wisely, that it might be better to start out with more modest goals, particularly as volume production of GRP panels was unknown territory. The target for '53 was a mere 300 cars, all of them Polo White. The following year it was hoped to produce—and sell—10,000.

**Opposite & Below:
The calm before the
storm.**

**The styling of the first
generation Corvette
reflects the residual
restraint of the early
'fifties, just before the
dawn of the
Rock&Roll era.**

The original Corvette assembly line was a mere six cars long, tucked away in a corner of the massive Chevrolet plant at Flint. The engines had to be brought in from the factory in Tonawanda, New York whilst the forty-six pieces that made up the body were produced by the Molded Fiber Glass Company of Ashtabula, Ohio. To begin with, inevitably, production was painfully slow and build-quality extremely variable. By the time production was shifted to a purpose-built plant in St. Louis, Missouri, in 1954, a mere three cars a day were being completed. By the middle of that year, this figure had risen to six hundred cars a month, with a choice of colors: Polo White with red interior; Pennant Blue Metallic with tan interior and Sportsman Red with red and white interior. A very small number of cars, probably about half a dozen, were painted black and had a red interior. The cars came with 6.70 × 15 whitewall tires, a recirculating, hot water heater and a Delco signal-seeking radio. Instrumentation included a clock and a tachometer that read to 5000rpm. Output was moving steadily upwards towards a target of a thousand a month when it was realized that supply was outstripping demand.

The high price had put the Corvette out of reach of the youthful market at which it was aimed. To try to rectify this, the 1954 model was marked down to $2774. Potential customers lured by the attractive new price were surprised to discover that the only transmission available was listed as an option, as were the windshield wipers and the heater. The true price was, in fact, $3250. Road testers agreed that the Corvette was neither a racer nor a cruiser. Production was halted at 3640 and by the end of the year nearly 1500 of those were still sitting in dealers' showrooms.

Left & Below: Initial sales were slow but Chevrolet did their best to bring the product to the people with the *Corvette Cavalcade*, here seen traversing the L.A. Harbor Freeway and Chicago's Lake Shore Drive.

This Page: The 1954 Motorama, Corvette-based Corvair never went into production. A decade later, GM must have wished that the car that bore the name hadn't either.

Following Page: In addition to Polo White, 1954 Corvette buyers could have their cars finished in hot Sportsman Red or this cool, Pennant Blue.

Right & Following Page: The plate says it all, or most of it. '55 brought a 265 cid V8 motor, three-speed, manual transmission and a top speed of close to 120mph. Note the enlarged V in CheVrolet on the front fender, indicating the new V8 engine.

1954 also saw the birth of Ford's Thunderbird, which would go on sale the following year. This was also a two-seater, and based on an identical, 102-in. wheelbase. It was described, enigmatically, as a "Personal Car" and offered, from the outset, with a V8 engine and a choice of either manual or automatic transmission. The T-Bird was far more luxuriously appointed than the Corvette but still managed, at $2994, to undercut its "real" price substantially. Ford had planned their new model meticulously, having conducted market research over a period of years. The Thunderbird was produced in big numbers from the outset, and Ford's confidence was not misplaced. In the first full year of production, 16155 Thunderbirds were sold against a measly 700 Corvettes. GM had already decided to continue production and the arrival of this upstart from their arch-enemy served only to stiffen their resolve to make the Corvette the car it really wanted to be. The arrival of another inspired engineer, this time from Europe, would help to rectify the situation. Zora Arkus-Duntov set to work, trying to fix the exhaust blow-back problem and the poor handling. Chief engineer Ed Cole picked up a project from his predecessor, E. H. Kelley, in the shape of the now legendary small-block V8. Originally intended to have a capacity of 231 cu.ins—smaller than what was officially termed the "Blue Flame" six fitted in the Corvette—Cole had the capacity increased to 265 cu.ins. He also reworked the cylinder heads, concentrating on efficient gas flow and better combustion. The V8 was 300lbs lighter than the Stovebolt and a remarkably compact unit, with lightweight valve-gear and much thinner cylinder walls and water jacket than was current Detroit practice. A short-stroke crankshaft allowed the engine to rev to 6000rpm.

In its standard state of tune, as fitted to Chevrolet sedans, this engine would produce up to 170bhp. When employed in

Below: Styling
revision is a constant
process. Here, louvers
in the front fenders on
a '55 show car
anticipate the gills of
the Mako of '68.

the Corvette, it was fitted with a four-barrel carburetor and
dual exhausts and produced 195bhp at 5000rpm. Maximum
torque was 260lb. ft. at 3000rpm. This brought the 0–60
acceleration time down from eleven seconds to under nine.
Styling revision was limited to an oversize, gold V in

CheVrolet, as inscribed on the front fenders, and a broadening of the radiator grille. There were still no roll-up windows or exterior door handles and sales remained low at 674, but ninety-nine percent of buyers were opting for the V8 motor.

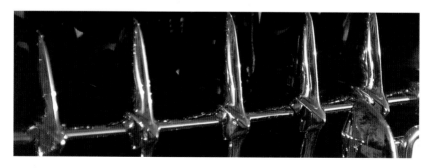

Previous Page & Right: Earl's styling on the first generation Corvette may not have been 100% ergonomic, but the overall effect is one of perfect unanimity and concord.

1956–1957
First of the Fuelies

Left: The restyled
body of 1956 was
ravishing, combining
modernity and
classicism in a
perfectly balanced
package.

Below: The signature
fender "coves"
recalled the coach-
building of the inter-
war period. This detail
was dubbed the
LeBaron sweep.

To compliment the new V8 power plant, the Corvette's body
was radically restyled for 1956. Still constructed in fiberglass,
this would be the last model to be designed in Detroit before
the design department was relocated to GM's new Technical
Center at Warren, Michigan. The styling was based on an
amalgam of Motorama show cars from '55: the Chevrolet
Biscayne and a pair of designs known as LaSalle II. The
Biscayne featured an interior color-keyed to its paint job, with
parking lights in the fenders and a grille composed of vertical
bars. The LaSalles – a roadster and a coupe, featured a detail
that would become the distinguishing feature of the second
generation Corvette: the cove. This was a tapered, concave
depression in the body sides that curved back from the front
wheel arches into the doors. It was described as echoing the
LeBaron Sweep, an allusion to the coach-built automobiles of
the 'twenties and 'thirties. The cove was outlined in chrome
and usually painted in a contrasting color. The effect was
magnificent; the restyled '56 Corvette was a superb-looking

automobile. The wire stone guards on
the headlamps were abandoned, having
been discovered to be illegal in some
states; the rear lights were faired neatly
into the fenders and the body shape
was subtly reworked to give a more
purposeful appearance. The spinners
on the hub caps were still phony, as
were the intake scoops that sprouted
from the front fenders just ahead of the
doors, but overall the improvement
was huge. Beneath the surface, Ed Cole
continued to push ahead with
mechanical improvements. The two-
speed, Powerglide transmission passed
away, unmourned, to be replaced by a
standard three-speed manual shift.
Performance was now truly in the
sports car class; the Corvette went as
well as it looked, at last. Duntov had
been at work on the camshaft profiles
and this, coupled with a four-barrel
carburetor and a compression ratio of
9.25:1 boosted output to 225bhp @
5200rpm, with 270lb. ft. of torque @
3600rpm. The clutch was beefed up to
cope with the increased power and the
rear axle ratio set at 3.55:1, with

Left: 1956: The radiator is
reassuringly familiar, the rest
is refreshingly different.

Top: This full-scale prototype is fitted with the optional hardtop, first glimpsed on Motorama cars back in 1954.

Right: The instrument layout is still rather haphazard, but at least there are now roll-up windows.

3.27:1 as an option. In standard form, with the three-speed box, a '56 Corvette could record a 0–60 time of around seven and a half seconds and run a standing quarter in sixteen, with a terminal speed in excess of 90mph. Top speed was close on 120mph. Despite continuing concerns over brake fade and understeer, the Corvette's road manners were becoming a lot more civilized. Weight distribution was now 52/48, front to rear, and the steering geared to three and a half turns, lock to lock. The price was pegged at $3170 and there was an optional hard-top, based on a '54 show model, plus a transistorized radio—for '56 was the year of Rock and Roll, notably via Alan Freed and CBS. The range of colors now available included Polo White, Onyx Black, Venetian Red,

Below: The hood line is now much neater but somehow the car looks strangely unfinished without the outlining of the side coves.

Cascade Green, Shoreline Beige, and Silver. Best of all, there were wind-up windows! Production leapt from less than 700 to 3467.

Just as Harley Earl and Ed Cole had put their heart and soul into the Corvette project, and laid their reputations on the line for that Grand Original, the plastic bath tub of 1953, so Zora Arkus-Duntov, who came to GM in that very year, at the tender age of 43, was to follow suit. The Corvette became his pride and his passion and he played with it, magnificently, for twenty years. Duntov had been born in Belgium in 1909 and educated in Petrograd (formerly St. Petersburg, subsequently Leningrad and eventually St. Petersburg, again) until the Russian revolution, when the family returned to Germany, where he graduated in Mechanical Engineering. The Duntovs had to move again, this time to Paris, to escape the menace of the rise of the Nazis in Germany. In the 'thirties, Duntov made a name for himself as an expert in supercharging but he also had a profitable side-line: gold smuggling. The technique was to conceal coins in the axle sleeve of a Ford V8 and drive, under cover of darkness, for the Belgian border. On long, downhill stretches, the twenty-year-old motor would rev to around 6000 and then run out of steam. Duntov designed an overhead valve conversion which doubled the engine's output. On arrival in the United States he and his brother, Yura, established Ardun Mechanical, in Brooklyn, and put the conversion, known as the Ardun Head, into production. In the immediate post-war years he worked as a consultant to both Porsche and Mercedes-Benz in Germany and to Allard, who employed Cadillac engines, in England. By late 1952 he was back in America and in the spring of the following year, just before the first production Corvette rolled off the line at Flint, he had finally arrived where he belonged – in the bosom of The General.

Right: Zora Arkus-Duntov, known as *Mister Corvette*, was an imaginative and innovative engineer whose devotion to the Corvette was positively passionate.

Duntov was a keen and accomplished racing driver. He took class wins in the Le Mans 24 hour race in 1954 and '55, driving a Porsche Spyder! In 1956, he managed to total a

Below: Duntov was a committed competition driver. Here, he's between Betty Skelton(left) and John Fita(right) at Daytona Beach in February, 1956. The Corvette has just established its 150mph record.

hardtop Corvette at the Milford proving ground, cracking one of his vertebrae in the process. This was right at the time when Harry Barr, who had succeeded Ed Cole as chief engineer at Chevrolet, was trying, with great difficulty, to perfect the Ramjet fuel-injection system for the Corvette. Duntov was obviously the man to solve the problem, but he was immobilized by a plaster cast that held his entire upper body rigid—he couldn't even put a pair of pants on. Such was

the spell that the Corvette cast however, over all those who came into intimate contact with it, that Duntov came back to work, where, for three months, he had to stand at his desk, wearing a skirt...

Ramjet was developed by Rochester Carburetor but was an in-house, General Motors design. The inlet manifold was formed in aluminum and fuel was carefully metered via a high pressure pump that was driven direct from the distributor.

Below: Duntov shows
how it's done at
Daytona - NASCAR
Speed Week, 1956.

Left: 1957 brought optional Ramjet fuel-injection, with appropriate badging to distinguish the cars so equipped.

Below: Ramjet was effective, when it worked. Early set-ups were notoriously temperamental.

The fuel-injection option was only available on the new-for-'57, 283 cu.in. V8. With the Ramjet, this engine achieved the elusive one horsepower per cubic inch output in a volume-production unit that had been the goal of auto engineers for decades. The system suffered from a lot of problems in the early days, notably due to dirt getting into the fuel lines—probably from the fuel itself—and uneven running due to the injectors getting overheated. Of

Top Left: The 283cid V8 was new for '57. Output, without fuel-injection, was still an impressive 220bhp.

the 6339 Corvettes built in 1957, a mere 240 were fitted with the Ramjet system, but this gave them performance that was, especially in the 'fifties, nothing short of awesome. An optional four-on-the-floor gear shift was introduced at a mere $188 extra. The four-speed gear box, designed by Chevrolet and built by Borg Warner, had its additional gear interposed between first and second on the three speed, thus producing a "close-ratio" box, of the kind beloved of enthusiastic drivers. Coupled to a Ramjet equipped V8 and driving through the optional 4.11:1 rear axle, the Corvette could hit 60mph in 5.7 seconds, 100mph in a little under 17 seconds and cover a

Top Right: Handsome
is as handsome does.
By 1957 it was hard
to tell whether the
Corvette went as
well as it looked and
looked as good as
it went.

quarter mile from a standing start in 14.3 seconds, reaching a
speed of 96mph. Top speed was 132mph.

Duntov realized that this "second generation" Corvette
would need some serious revision in the suspension, braking and
steering departments to deal with all those extra horses. His
efforts finally resulted in the introduction of the Regular
Production Option (RPO) 684 suspension package. This
included a front anti-roll bar, up-rated springs and shock-
absorbers, ceramic/metallic brake linings in finned and ventilated
drums, Positraction limited-slip differential and a steering
modification that reduced lock-to-lock turns from 3.7 to 2.9.

There were three rear axle ratio options: 3.70:1, 4.11:1 and 4.56:1. With all the goodies, the '57 Corvette was effectively a street-legal race car. To demonstrate this, a pair of production models were the first GT Class cars to finish at Sebring that year, in 12th and 15th places. The 12th placed car finished no less than 20 laps ahead of the top placed Mercedes Benz 300SL, which had been, up to that point, "regarded as the world's fastest road car."

The Sebring victory was a watershed for the Corvette. It had earned the respect of the most critical of judges and been proved in the heat of competition. In '56, the Corvette had finished first in the Sports Car Club of America's national production car championship and this was repeated in '57. The Corvette's future was assured, even though it was still to show a profit for Chevrolet. Sadly, no sooner had the Corvette shown its ability to dominate the race track than General Motors signed up to the Automobile Manufacturers Association agreement to withdraw official support from motor racing. This was due to pressure from the National Safety Council, which claimed that using recognizable road cars on the track, and referring to their race-bred qualities in advertising material had a detrimental effect on the behavior of the purchasers of such cars on the public highway. No manufacturer wanted to be seen to be promoting reckless driving, and so support for competition was totally withdrawn. The effect of this enforced shift of emphasis was to become noticeable in the Corvette's evolution over the next few years.

Top Left: Exclusive and exciting, the '57 Corvette offered the best of both worlds.

Right: The Corvette was campaigned competitively throughout the 'fifties with spectacular success. This is a specially-prepared, experimental SR-Z of 1957.

Next Page: Suave, sophisticated, sporting and sexy. The '57 Corvette just about had it all.

1958–1962
More Chrome – More Horses

The overwhelming success of the Corvette as a race car during the '57 season caused Ford to finally throw in the towel and make the Thunderbird a full four-seater in 1958.

Ironically, withdrawal from racing shifted the focus of the Corvette's development from go to show. Harley Earl was now approaching the end of his long and distinguished career at GM and would finish with a flourish that was typical of the man: the towering, 42 inch fins of the '59 Cadillac. The Corvette received a dose of juke-box style as well, though it didn't suit it quite so much. Quad headlamps were introduced, a heavier grille and liberal applications of chrome, notably to the rear, where accent lines ran up from the inner edges of the back bumper and across the deck lid. Dummy louvers appeared on the bonnet, along with non-functional air intakes behind the heavy front bumpers and phony vents in the side coves, embellished with yet more chrome accents. Chrome strips also ran back from the headlamps, along the top of the front fenders. The '58 rode the same wheelbase as the '57 but was 2.3ins. wider and nearly 10ins. longer. All this added was weight, which went, at the very least, from 2730lbs. to 2793lbs.: sixty-three pounds of excess fat that could, with options, rise to nearly 200lbs. This was after the car had actually got lighter, down from 2764lbs. in '56.

Left: The chrome embellishments on the '58 Corvette were more of an imposition than an improvement.

Below: The new, improved, dash panel layout is very clearly visible in this '58 interior mock-up.

One of the few improvements, at the request of Duntov, was an overhaul of the dashboard layout that grouped all the instruments in front of the driver in a binnacle, rather than having them spread, impressively but illegibly, across the width of

the fascia. Driver and passenger got the benefit of seat belts as standard and the passenger got a grab handle as well. The Ramjet fuel-injection system had been further refined to give greater reliability and output rose to 290bhp @ 6200rpm.

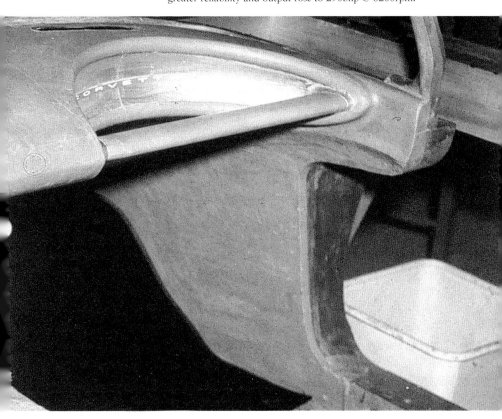

Below: Giving the people what they want, the Corvette's sales continued to rise steadily through the late '50s.

Carburetor models produced up to 270bhp and, despite the official ban on promoting racing, or even the thought of racing, the up-rated race suspension package was retained as an option.

The heavy-handed styling of the '58 Corvette looks, to the modern eye, like a retrograde step, but Harley Earl's appraisal

of the American public's taste was very rarely wrong. Even in the poor economic climate, production rose to 9168. Sales were up almost forty per cent on '57 and an incredible hundred and fifty per cent on '56. The Corvette moved, for the first time, into profit.

Experience based on experiment: the styling of the
Corvette was, and ever has been, under constant review.
In these pictures, from 1958 – 1960, we can see the
extent to which both Harely Earl, and subsequently Bill
Mitchell, were willing to dare to be different.

Duntov and his engineers did their best to counteract the best efforts of the Styling Shop, continuing to refine the suspension set-up, with even harder settings on the RPO 684 option. RPO 686 (sintered metallic brake linings) was introduced, for a modest $27, and radius arms were introduced into the rear suspension in an effort to reduce axle-tramp during hard cornering and torque effect under acceleration. Meanwhile, the styling was tidied up.

Right: In black and white, the interior of this '59 looks postitively restrained.

Below: Even in carbureted form, by 2959, the 283 cu.in. V8 could produce around 270bhp.

The dummy louvers disappeared from the hood and the chrome accents were deleted from the trunk. The wheel trims were redesigned to allow more cooling to the brake drums. The '59 Corvette, in standard trim, could easily accelerate to 60mph in under eight seconds and cover a quarter mile in around fifteen. That was fantastic performance in the 'fifties – it's far from disgraceful more than forty years on.

Harley Earl's retirement was announced on December 1, 1959. He had been with General Motors for thirty-two years and had, during that time, become the undisputed style arbiter of the American Automobile industry and thus, perhaps, the most influential designer of all time. His influence would linger; he had, of course, personally penned designs for the Corvette thru' 1961. He would be succeeded by his pupil, the forty-six-year-old William "Bill" Mitchell, who, like all good pupils, couldn't wait to have a crack at the teacher's job. The third generation Corvette, which Mitchell was to make his own, was still three years away in the metal, but was already taking shape on the drawing board. The shift would be incremental but the end result would be totally radical.

Complex as it is, the detailing of the '59 comes together extremely well.

Like its predecessors, the '59 Corvette managed to be both Beauty and The Beast at the same time.

Next Page: Harley Earl retired in December, 1959, after over thirty years' service to GM. The fabulous styling of Corvette of that year is a fitting tribute to a true genius.

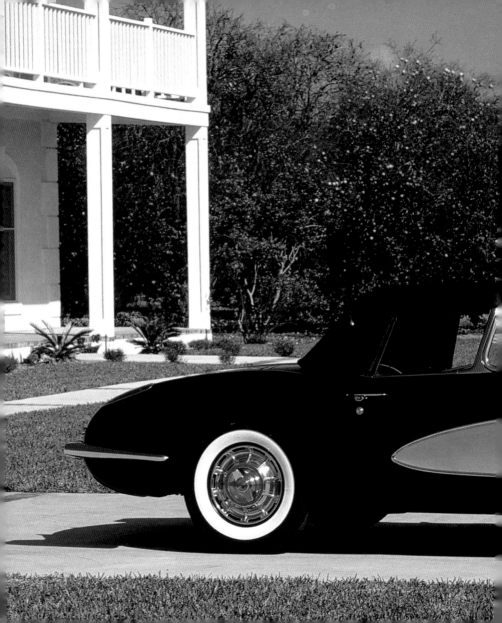

Right: A '59 Corvette
is a car to brighten
the dullest day...

Next page: ...and
perfect for fun in
the sun!

Right: The XP-700 protoype of 1960 demonstrates that the styling department were hardly short of ideas. Not all of them made it through to production, however.

Left: As it enters the '60s, the Corvette is obviously just getting ready to swing.

Above: The restyled tail of the '61/'62 'Vette shows the influence of the XP-700.

Next Page: Juke-box styling reached its zenith—or its nadir, depending on your taste—with the '58/'59 Corvettes.

1960
Corvette

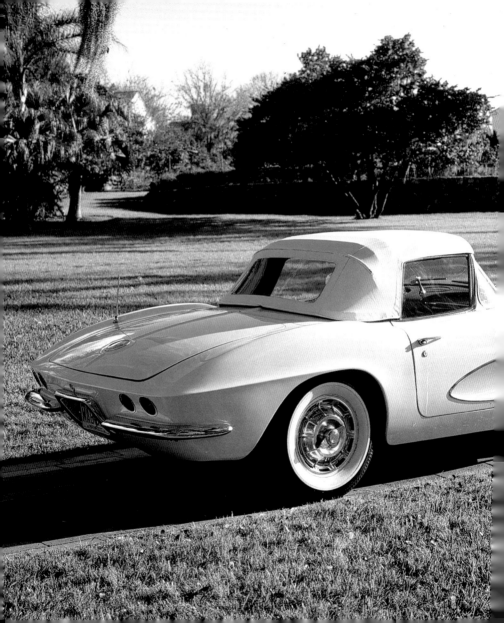

'61 saw the first real evidence of a new hand on the tiller. The reworking was subtle but the direction that the styling was being taken in was becoming ever more apparent. The tail section gave the clearest clues: the deck was flattened, losing its voluptuous curves and becoming sharper-edged—a distinct break with the 'fifties feel of the second generation models. Bill Mitchell had already created the XP700 show car and the racing Stingray (one word) and the '61 car showed the influence of both. Chrome was gently removed, the gleaming "teeth" of the radiator grille being replaced by a more subtle mesh. Underneath, the radiator was now crafted in aluminum. Interior refinements included dual sun visors, a warning light for the parking brake, and windshield washers. It's interesting to note that nearly ninety per cent of customers opted for manual transmission, and of those, two thirds wanted the four speed, now with an aluminum housing. A fully optioned 'Vette could now run a standing quarter in 14.2 seconds, hitting 99mph; 60mph could come up in 5.5 seconds and the top speed was close on 130mph.

Left: The "duck tail" rear of the '61/'62 restyle incorporated recessed, quad lamps that have become a Corvette trademark.

Styling revisions for '61 were mainly about simplification. A mesh grille replaced the chrome teeth—silencing one of the last echocs of the 1953 car.

Left: The Corvette has always been a fine example of good breeding, retaining its unique character from generation to generation.

Next page: Note the opening trunk lid, soon to disappear, and the instruments, now neatly grouped in front of the driver.

Right: Maximum output from the 283 cu.in. V8, boosted by fuel-injection—as in this fine example—was in excess of 300bhp.

Next Page: The beauty was more than skin deep, as its clutch, gearbox, suspension and steering had all been improved.

Above: The crisp, de-chromed lines of the re-worked '62 Corvette.

The 1962 Corvette is regarded as a classic among classics and is a true "watershed" car. It was the last to have benefited, directly, from the hand of Harley Earl. It was the last to utilize Bob McLean's cross-braced chassis design that dated from the 1953 original and was still going strong and coping with more than double the horsepower of the truck-engined, bus-tired original. The small-block V8, originally displacing 283 cu.ins. was bored out an eighth of an inch to 4 inches and had its stroke increased by a quarter of an inch to $3\frac{1}{4}$ inches, raising the capacity to 327 cu.ins. Maximum output, with fuel injection, was now 360bhp. The Corvette could now hit 100mph in a quarter of a mile from a standing start, covering the distance in 15 seconds, even without fuel-injection! Styling was sharpened up and toned down. Contrast-color coves were deleted—an abandonment of what was, perhaps, one of the earliest and most effective examples of "retro-styling," echoing the glamour of the 'thirties—in favor of a cleaner and more unified look that was to typify 'sixties style. As ever, the Corvette was showing the way. Ed Cole gave way to Semon E. "Bunkie" Knudsen as general manager and Corvette production rose to 14,531. Base price was $4038, rising to around $5500 for a fully loaded example. That meant that the buyer could have the performance of a Ferrari for under half the price and without the rust problems. Thanks to the combined efforts of Misterearl, Mister McLean, Mister Cole, Mister Curtice, Mister Keating, Mister Barr, Mister Duntov and Mister Mitchell, and others, the '62 Corvette was, effectively, unimprovable.

Above: The '62 Corvette has become a classic among classics —unlike the ill-fated Corvair in the background.

Right: Even though a completely new model was imminent, '62 sales shot to 14,531.

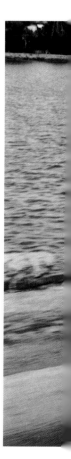

Where were you in sixty-two? The Corvette
looked great from every angle, most
especially from behind the wheel.

The '62 still looks cool after over forty years. Thanks to its rust-proof bodywork and bullet-proof engineering, a surprising number of them are still around to be admired.

Right & Next Page: The shape of things to come. The rear view of the '62 is very close to that of its successor, the Sting Ray. The trunk lid is the main giveaway!

As ever, the Corvette was equally at home or road and track. Here we see a '62 parked quietly in the drive, while Dick Thompson takes his to the SCCAA Prod championship.

1963–1967
Sting Ray! Sting Ray!

When something can't be made any better the only thing to do is make something better. Bunkie Knudsen was a second generation General Motors man. His dad, William Knudsen, had been made head of operations at Chevrolet back in 1922, when K. W. Zimmerschied moved to the post of assistant to the president of the company, then Pierre du Pont. William was known as "Hurry Up" Knudsen in recognition of his enthusiasm for production. It was during Knudsen's reign, in 1927, that Chevrolet's valve-in-head, "Stovebolt" six-cylinder engine, which would, of course, eventually power the first Corvette, went into production. On the tenth anniversary of that model's introduction, a totally new car was to be offered to the public. By now, the Corvette was perceived as a separate

Right: The Sting Ray was one of the first cars in the world to benefit from wind-tunnel testing to improve aero-dynamics. Full scale mock-ups like this one were employed so that adjustments could be made prior to production.

Above: The styling of the Sting Ray drew heavily on Bill Mitchell's Mako Shark styling exercise—seen here with plexi-glass hard top—of 1961.

entity from run-of-the-mill Chevrolets and so to distinguish the all-new model from its predecessors it was given an additional title: Sting Ray. Much has been made of the likelihood of the name having been derived from Bill Mitchell's fondness for fishing trips, and the styling does have certain undeniably piscatorial elements. Mitchell had shown his beautiful Mako Shark concept car in '61, anticipating many of the features that would appear on later production Sting Rays. It seems most likely, however, that the inspiration for the Stingray racer's styling came not from a fish but from a cat. Jaguar had wowed the world with their beautiful E-Type (XKE) in 1961, but the car had first appeared as a racing prototype in 1956. The production E-Type was a road-going development of the C-Type and D-Type racers which had performed spectacularly at LeMans and elsewhere. The D-Type, along with its even more glamorous stable mate, the XKSS, provided much of the

Above Left: The SS Racer underwent as many revisions as the road models, serving as a rolling test bed and, in the process, reaching 183mph.

inspiration for the Corvette SS racer, which received a favorable review from Juan Manuel Fangio, probably the greatest race-car driver of all time, after he tried it out at Sebring in 1957. The SS inspired the Stingray race-car which in turn inspired the XP-720. The XP-720 became the '63 Sting Ray. It is worth noting, in support of this argument, that Mitchell himself drove an E-Type Jaguar…

Above: Family likeness is seen in the tail treatment of the all-new Sting Ray.

Like the Jaguar, the new Corvette was offered in both convertible and coupe form. The look of the car also echoed Larry Shinoda's "Q" car styling essays, but it was from the XP-720 that Duntov developed the Sting Ray's ladder-frame

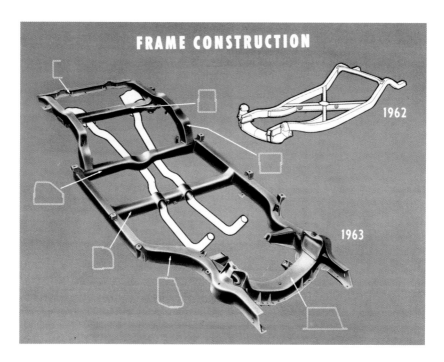

FRAME CONSTRUCTION

1962

1963

Above: Duntov's "Ladder-Frame" chassis allowed the new car to sit lower on the road than the original X-Frame.

chassis and suspension layout. Taking the XP-720 chassis, with its five cross-members, as his template, Duntov had the passenger compartment positioned as far back as was feasible and the center of gravity lowered from nineteen to sixteen and a half inches. Ground clearance would be a mere five inches. All this, combined with the independent rear suspension that Duntov was adamant about including, would ensure an enviable combination of secure road holding and excellent ride quality. The 102 inch wheelbase of the original roadster—also

Right: The Sting Ray was beautifully balanced, to the eye and on the road.

Below: The Sting Ray's GRP shell was subjected to lengthy stress-testing prior to being put into production.

echoing a Jaguar: the XK120—was cut back to 98 inches. The drive-train was routed right down the center line and kept as low as possible. Weight distribution was almost perfect at 51/49 per cent.

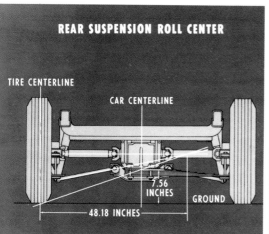

REAR SUSPENSION ROLL CENTER

TIRE CENTERLINE

CAR CENTERLINE

7.56 INCHES

GROUND

48.18 INCHES

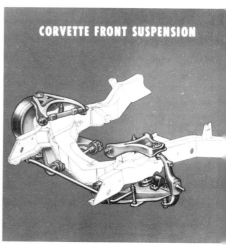

CORVETTE FRONT SUSPENSION

Above: Duntov insisted on independent rear suspension for the Sting Ray—and he got his way.

In order to justify the cost of the rear suspension, which was fiercely resisted by the GM management, Duntov assured the suits that its inclusion would help to push sales towards 30,000. His confidence was justified. In the first year of production, almost 22,000 Sting Rays found homes, the coupe and the convertible being equally favored.

Again like the Jaguar, the Corvette was among the first road cars to benefit from serious attention being paid to its aerodynamics. In the mid-fifties the D-Type, shaped by Malcolm Sayer, could run to 180mph with a (comparatively) long-stroke, six cylinder engine of 3.4 liters (210 cu.ins.). Wind tunnel testing had as much as anything to do with determining the Corvette's basic shape. Despite the fact that there was more steel and less GRP in the new car, kerb weight was down a little on the '62. Oddly, neither version had a trunk lid, so

Fitted with the Turbo Fire 327, a '63 Corvette could achieve speeds in excess of 150mph. Competition options could improve both speed and handling dramatically. The chequered flag badge now seemed wholly appropriate.

Above: A full-size, painted mock-up of the Stingray is rolled out into the daylight for appraisal.

Opposite Top: The beautiful proportions of Mitchell's design are shown clearly in this overhead view.

Opposite: Pop-up headlights were standard and would become a Corvette hallmark. Genuine knock-off hubs were an optional extra.

access to the luggage compartment was via the cockpit. It can't have been much fun trying to slot a heavy suitcase behind the seats but there was compensation, perhaps, in the car's ravishing, unbroken lines. The most celebrated detail of the coupe was its "spine." This was a continuous line that ran from the tip of the tapering bulge in the hood to the center of the deck, bisecting the rear window on the way—like the tail of a stingray… Nobody liked it at the time, now it's considered classic. It is, if nothing else, concrete evidence of Mr. Mitchell's corporate clout. The elegant side coves were gone, but a ghostly reminder of them remained in the shape of a pair of dummy vents on each front fender. A smart, lift-off hardtop was supplied for the roadster, and the coupe's doors cut into the roofline to make entry and exit from the low-slung cockpit easier and more decorous—short skirts were fashionable in the 'sixties, remember?

The steering still used a recirculating ball system but was a new design that gave tighter response. There were still quad headlamps, but they now hid themselves away when not in use. The lights were raised by electric motors when switched on. Brakes were now self-adjusting; an alternator was fitted in place of a generator. The car had an alloy clutch housing and a lightweight flywheel. For the first time, a full leather interior was offered. Competition was back on the agenda and a host of mouth-watering options were offered with this in mind. These included up-rated suspension, including heavy-duty torsion bars, Al-Fin aluminum brake drums, metallic brake linings and cast alloy wheels with knock-off hubs. A thirty-six and a half gallon fuel tank was also available, which presumably occupied most of the luggage space that was inaccessible anyway.

The '63 Sting Ray was the fastest and best handling Corvette to date. Fitted with a 3.70:1 rear axle, a '63 Corvette tested by Sports Car Graphic recorded a 0–60mph time of 5.6 seconds and a standing quarter-mile time of 14.1 seconds with a terminal speed of 102mph. Top speed was measured at 151mph. Forty years on, that's still impressive. Carroll Shelby was instrumental in having a number of Corvettes bodied in aluminum by Scaglietti in Italy, in an attempt to produce a lightweight, racing derivative. He ended up putting a Ford motor into a space frame chassis from AC Motors of Thames Ditton, thus producing the legendary Cobra, which, though it often bettered the Sting Ray on the track, could never hope to catch it in the market place. The '63 Sting Ray was the only truly "original" Corvette between the 1953 original and the

Below: Roger Penske campaigned the mighty Grand Sport at Daytona and Nassau in '63. The car was uncatchable.

sixth-generation model of 1984. Duntov's chassis and suspension layout, that he'd had to go to battle with the management over, would last—and improve—for over twenty years. By now, the AMA's anti-race rulings were a thing of the past and Chevrolet started work on a competition racer to take on the Cobra. The Grand Sport was fitted with a specially built, 377 cu.in. aluminum V8. GM got cold feet and only five cars were produced, but all three of the ones that ran at Daytona in '63 ran ten seconds a lap faster than the Cobras. At Nassau, in the same year, Roger Penske won a Grand Sport. Had General Motors stuck with the project and produced the 100 plus units that were necessary for the Grand Sport to be classified as a production car it would have, without doubt, have been a world beater.

Below: Despite the disapproval of the AMA, a lot of '63 Sting Rays seemed to be out on the race track shortly after delivery.

Above: Mitchell's Sting Ray racer, dating from the late '50s, slowly mutated into the '63 road car.

Right: The Grand Sport racer was intended to beat the Ford powered AC Cobra, and so it did. At Daytona, in '63, the Sting Ray was ten seconds a lap faster.

Above: With looks
like this, a choice
between roadster and
coupe body styles,
and shattering
performance, it's
hardly surprising that
'63 Corvette sales
passed 20,000.

1964 brought yet more power to production
modes. Work on the ports and valve gear and a re-
profiled cam with greater life and longer dwell raised
the output of the fuel-injected engine to 375bhp @
6200rpm. The suspension was subtly adjusted to
improve the ride without compromising the handling.
Non-porous alloy wheels were now available and a
host of minor revisions were made to the interior,
including matt-black, anti-glare instrument bezels. The
biggest change to the exterior was the deletion of the
split rear window, thus ensuring the '63's collector
value to the end of time.

1964 saw the birth of the Ford Mustang. Like the
original Corvette, the first Mustangs came with a six
cylinder engine as basic spec though a V8 was available
from the outset. Ford scored a victory in the 1964 Tour
de France and had numerous other events, but the
Mustang, with its four seats, was represented by Ford
as a "tourer" and raced as a saloon car.

Right: Mitchell's central spine styling motif, which divided the rear window, lasted for one year only, making the '63 Sting Ray an instant collector's piece.

Note that neither the roadster nor the coupe now had a trunk lid. Luggage had to be loaded from the inside of the car— tough for golfers.

Right: Most of the styling revisions for '64 were minor, but mechanical refinements and improvements came thick and fast.

Right: '64 front end styling is unchanged from '63...

Left: ...but the deletion of the center spine from the rear window gives the car a more open feel and improves rear visibility.

Next page: His 'n' Hers sixty-fours.

American sports cars all look alike.
'65 CORVETTE

Corvette is America's one true sports car—has been for years.

But Corvette is also two body styles. Five engines and three transmissions available. Plus enough other equipment you can order to make any kind of sports car you want.

For aficionados, there's the snarly Corvette. Ordered with a 375-hp Ram-jet fuel-injected V8, 4-speed fully synchronized shift, Positraction, cast aluminum wheels, special goldwall tires, genuine wood-rimmed steering wheel, telescopic steering column,

special front and rear suspension and special exhaust system.

For boulevardiers, there's the plush Corvette. Ordered with a 300-hp V8, Powerglide, power brakes, steering and windows, tinted glass, genuine leather seat trim, AM/FM radio, and air conditioning.

And if you're a bit of both aficionado and boulevardier, you can get all kinds of in-between Corvettes, part snarly and part plush.

Every Corvette gives you 4-wheel disc brakes, fully independent suspen-

sion, retractable headlights, and a sumptuous bucket-seated interior as standard. At a very reasonable price compared to any car near its class.

Now you know why America has only one sports car; with all those different Corvette versions, who needs any more?

Corvette Sting Ray

CHEVROLET

Chevrolet Division of General Motors, Detroit, Michigan

Left: Chevrolet's advertising underlines the point that there is only one, true, American sports car.

Below: A big block V8 was available for '65, starting out at 396 cu. ins. and producing up to 425bhp.

The Corvette, on the other hand, was becoming more uncompromisingly sporting in character year on year. In 1965, for the first time, all-round disc brakes were offered, as a "delete option" which meant that the customer could save all of $64.50 by opting for drums instead. 316 buyers chose to do this, out of a total of 23,562: 1.3 per cent.

'65 saw another major innovation: the adoption of a "big block" V8. The "W" motor had been employed in Chevrolet saloons for five years. Starting out at 348 cu.ins., its capacity had steadily climbed to a massive 427 cu.ins. and become known as the Z-II. There was, however, a second 427 engine,

landard wheel cover

rap-over door

Outside rearview mirror

The '65 Corvette, full on and in detail. Note how the doors cut into the roofline to allow easier access, but the luggage compartment has no access at all!

which Chevrolet had used in the '63 NASCAR racing season. The largest of a series of four engines, it was known simply as the Mark IV, but when put into the Corvette it was re-christened the Turbo Jet. It was company policy that "medium-sized" cars, into which category the Corvette fell, should not be fitted with engines displacing over 400 cu.ins. The 427 was duly sleeved down to 396 cu.ins. With a four-barrel carburetor, solid lifters and a compression ration of 11:1, the engine produced 425bhp @ 6400rpm and 425lb. ft. of torque at 4000rpm. To handle this kind of power, a new and more robust four-speed gearbox had been introduced the previous year. With more widely-spaced ratios, stronger synchromesh and a smoother shift action than the Borg-Warner original that it replaced, this item was produced at the GM plant in Muncie, Indiana, and became known, affectionately, as the Muncie Box. The suspension was beefed up, naturally, with stiffer torsion bars front and rear. Similarly, a heavier clutch was fitted, along with an increased capacity cooling system. Despite the additional weight of the new engine, Duntov managed to keep the balance of the car perfect, maintaining a 51/49 per cent front to rear ratio. Styling continued to be simplified, decoration was shed and the lines got cleaner and cleaner as time went by.

Although the Sting Ray was gaining ever more power and sophistication mechanically, the exterior styling became even simpler and more serene.

The big block engine necessitated a massive "power bulge" in the hood and side-mounted "shotgun" exhaust pipes were offered as an option for those who felt the need. Elliott M. "Pete" Estes replaced Bunkie Knudsen as Chevrolet's general manager in 1965 but the Corvette just went on, from strength to strength.

Below: The 396 "Turbo Jet" had been sleeved down from 427 cu.ins., but would regain its lost cubes before long.

All round disc brakes were now offered at a very reasonable $64.50. Lap seat belts were provided, but not always worn, apparently.

Previous page: The '65 Sting Ray's front fender vents recalled the "gills" of the Mako Shark and would become a Corvette hallmark.

Above: Both interior and exterior detailing was distinctive, but remarkably restrained for the period.

Left: The fitting of the big block V8 had necessitated the creation of a very genuine, ventilated "power bulge" in the hood.

1966
There's no Substitute for Cubes...

This phrase has long been regarded, by mostly envious Europeans, as an example of American lack of refinement, but it is, in fact, merely a paraphrase of a remark made by one W. O. Bentley, "If you want more power, build a bigger engine." Nobody ever accused Bentley of vulgarity, did they?. Whatever, in 1966 the Corvette went the whole nine yards. Duntov introduced the Mark IV engine restored to its full 427 cu.in. capacity. In order to avoid problems with insurers, Chevrolet deliberately *under*-quoted the Corvette's maximum power output, leaving it, without explanation, unchanged at a "mere" 425bhp. The true figure was probably around 450.

Depending on the axle ratios, a Big Block Corvette could accelerate to 60mph in under 4.8 seconds and still have a top speed of 140mph. With higher gearing, upwards of 160mph was easily achievable.

The 427 Corvette was half a ton heavier than the Shelby Cobra, with around the same horsepower, so it was less than a threat to the Ford-powered AC in the SCCA A-Production class—as if the Cobra was ever a "production" car—but the 'Vette could still win laurels in endurance racing. Penske's team ran 12th overall in the GT Class at the 1966 Daytona Continental.

Previous Page: The Mako Shark II remains one of the most striking automobile designs of all time and would provide the inspiration for the next generation of Corvettes.

Left: Styling was progressively simplified through '66 and '67, revealing how beautiful the lines of the Sting ray were.

Next Page: The side-mounted exhaust was an optional extra that seems superfluous today.

A new model was slated for the '67 but the body shape had caused problems in the wind tunnel and so Duntov decided to postpone its introduction for a year. This meant that 1967 was the final year for the Sting Ray but it turned out to be its greatest. On the track, Penske's team placed first at Sebring. On the road, the Corvette was taken back to its most beautiful basics, stylewise, by the total elimination of extraneous decoration, though a massive air-scoop was necessary on the hoods of cars fitted with the 427 V8. A reversing light was a unique feature on the '67 Corvette, as was the centrally mounted handbrake. A sign of the times was the fact that the hard-top was available with a black vinyl covering. The real highlight, however, was the production of around 20 L-88s. The L-88 chassis was equipped with the F-41 suspension package plus massive brakes and the Positraction differential. This version of the 427, running on high-octane fuel, could produce a mind-boggling 560bhp.

Previous Pages: Fuel injection on the small-block was deleted in '66; the carb'd 427 was cheaper and more powerful.

Left: By 1967, the last year of its life, the Corvette's stying had been pared back to the point where it resembled a designer's outline.

The 427 cu.ins. V8 approached 450bhp, giving a '67 Sting Ray so equipped better performance than many contemporary exotics. Acceleration was incredible, with sixty miles per hour coming up in under five seconds.

Once again, as in '62, a Corvette design would be abandoned at the peak of perfection. It's hard to see how the '67 could have been further improved. Note the reversing light— what else was there to add? A trunk lid, maybe?

Sting Ray sales had peaked in 1965 at 26,171 and even in '67, when the model was supposed to have been replaced, they were still over 23,000. In total, 120,000 Sting Rays had been sold, of which 72,500 were roadsters. The Sting Ray was the shortest production run of any Corvette design but has become one of the most sought after. It gave Americans some of the most exciting motoring in history and banished the myth of the US being unable to produce a "real" sports car. The '67 Corvette was quicker and faster than the Ferrari Testarossa of 1992.

The fifth generation Corvette took its inspiration from the Mako Shark II show car of 1965, which was in turn derived from the XP775 experimental of 1961—so that model that followed the Sting Ray, in some ways predated it.

Left: The big block V8 seems to be weighing this '67 down somewhat.

Next Page: Without power bulges or side exhausts, the line of the small-block-equipped '67 Sting Ray is pure perfection.

Right: Development problems dogged the Sting Ray's successor, delaying its release by a year and thus allowing this exquisite automobile to enjoy an "Indian Summer" in 1967.

Below: '67 sales approached 23,000, despite a new model being imminent. General Motors had produced a particularly great automobile.

1968–1982
The Mako Generation

Shark infested waters...

Below: Having waited over a year to try out the striking new Corvette, unfortunately some reviewers concluded that it was unfit to test.

According to automotive legend, Bill Mitchell, on one of his fishing trips, caught a shark. This was reputedly on the island of Bimini, in the Bahamas, some time in 1961. His XP-775 experimental, Corvette-based styling exercise of 1961, conducted in association with Larry Shinoda, is obviously predator-inspired. With its gill-like vents, pointed nose, gray-fade paint-job and all-around menacing aspect, it was christened the Mako Shark; all it needed to complete the illusion was fins—but this was the 'sixties already! The

production car that followed almost immediately, however, was called the Corvette Sting Ray and the ridge that ran from its nose to its tail was definitely more ray than shark. The car also took styling clues from another manufacturer, as had already been discussed. Mitchell's macho/mako musings continued through the single-seat XP-15 to the Mako Shark II of 1965.

The Mako Shark II caused a sensation at the '65 New York International Auto Show. Whereas the original Mako Shark had drawn on existing Corvette styling details, the Mako Shark II was a totally new concept, with a flowing fender line and a pinched waist, giving it the now familiar and classic "coke bottle" shape. Concealed lights were retained and complimented by concealed windshield wipers that eventually found their way onto production cars, briefly. The Mako Shark II had digital instrumentation and a rear window with electrically operated louvers that somehow added to the sub-aquatic effect. With its sinister, ground-hugging profile, the car drew huge crowds and much admiring comment when it was shown in the style capitals of Europe, including London, Paris and Turin.

Below: The Mako II's lines are still there, but aerodynamics had caused big problems.

Opposite: From some angles, the '68 Corvette is distinctly reminiscent of certain Ferrari models.

Top Left: The interior was cramped, due to to the "wasp waisted" body styling.

Top Right: Vents in the front fenders were practical rather than decorative, as they helped to correct a nasty tendency for the nose to lift.

Unfortunately, the styling of the Mako Shark II was matched neither by its handling characteristics nor by its driver-friendliness. The transition from show car to production model was overseen by David Holls of the Chevrolet Studio. Utilizing the Duntov chassis from the '63 Sting Ray, the new body showed an alarming tendency to lift under acceleration. This was cured, or at least addressed, by cutting vents in the front fenders and by increasing the spring rates. Due to the wasp-waisted body design, the passenger compartment was narrow and cramped and the low roof line inevitably restricted head room. To add to the new model's birth pangs, Duntov had been hospitalized in New York and thus the development work was given over to the Chevrolet sedan team. Just as Bunkie Knudsen had boosted production by introducing a second work shift on the Corvette line, so his successor, "Pete" Estes, eager to emulate Knudsen's achievement, immediately initiated a third. This time, however, increased output would be demanded of an unfamiliar design, with unfortunate consequences.

The impressive styling of the fifth generation Corvettes was not matched by the build quality—at least on early examples.

Launch of the new Corvette was delayed a year. Despite the public's evident desire for a new model, '67 Corvette sales had dipped rather than dropped dramatically, from 27,720 to 22,940. The excitement caused by the Mako Shark II, coupled with the postponement of the new Corvette's release could confidently be believed to have increased the eager anticipation of potential customers. Sadly, even after the design had received

Right: A good proportion of Corvette drivers opted for the four-on-the-floor manual transmission option.

Below: Engine options included the mighty L-88, which was capable of producing 560bhp. Even the "base" 350 cu.ins. V8 now pushed out a respectable 300bhp.

an additional year's revision, the 1968 Corvette was still seriously under-developed when offered to the public. The car was greeted by the motoring press with reactions that ranged from apathy to hostility. It looked new and yet there was no new chassis and no new engines; *Road & Track* pointed out that the styling, which had seemed so radical in Mako Shark II form, now seemed derivative, resembling the Ferraris of some years earlier. The car was bigger and yet there was less room in it; it had been necessary to tilt the seats back, the angle increasing from 25 degrees to 33 degrees, to allow for the low roof line. This resulted not only in discomfort for both driver and passenger but also meant that they were continually sliding forwards. The ride was harsh, the cockpit was noisy and there was no luggage space. The Targa roof was replaced by a T-Top, which incorporated a central brace in an attempt to reduce body shake. The car's overall appearance was striking and yet the finish and detailing were poor; the concealed windshield wipers worked intermittently, at best; the body panels fitted very badly and the paint finish was amateurish. The hard top leaked, the engine was difficult to start and had a tendency to overheat... *Car & Driver* returned theirs, saying that it was unfit to road test.

Left: A T-Bar had to be inserted in the roof of the coupe, to counter chronic body shake.

Opposite Inset: The 'Vette's bloodline was clearly visible in much of the fifth generation's detailing.

Top Inset: Despite the availability of incredible engines like the L-88 and the ZL-1, the small-block remained the most popular choice, giving up to 350bhp output.

Left: The new Corvette was seven inches longer, but it had less room for either passsengers or luggage.

Back to the Future...

Zora Arkus-Duntov had risen from his sick bed to discover that his unofficial rank of Corvette Head of Design was no longer acknowledged and that he was now answerable to the very team that had failed so lamentably to develop the '68 into the refined and desirable production model that it ought to have been. Happily, at exactly this time, one John DeLorean, who was later to achieve world-wide notoriety due to another severely under-developed sports car, became General Manager at Chevrolet, replacing Pete Estes. DeLorean, to his eternal credit, immediately appointed Duntov to the official position of *Chief Engineer—Corvette*.

On the plus side, the Corvette was now fitted, exclusively, with all-round disc brakes and the buying public seemed unfazed by the poor publicity: the first year's sales total rose to 28,566. It was obvious, however, that further refinement and a lot more attention to quality control would be necessary if these sales were to be sustained.

Left: Mr. Duntov may be smiling, but his fifth generation Corvette of 1968 had come in for some vicious criticism.

More is less...

The new Corvette was lower than its predecessor but it was also longer, wider and heavier. Overall length had increased from 175 ins. to 182 ins. and most of this was due to the greatly increased overhang at the front—the wheelbase remained unaltered from the Sting Ray's 98 ins. Track increased at both front and rear, up from 56.5 ins. to 58.7 ins. and from 57.0 ins. to 59.4 ins. respectively. Weight increase was an overall 150 lbs., so that the car weighed in at around 3400 lbs. Chassis revisions were minor. The rear springs were stiffened to help to reduce nose lift under acceleration, and on big-block optioned cars the front coil rates were also increased. The rear roll center was lowered, which, coupled with the suspension tuning, further encouraged understeer, an acknowledged Corvette trait. Combined with the fitting of wider (7 in.) wheels, however, all this served to increase the car's cornering limit from 0.75g to 0.84g. By 1969, critical comments were becoming marginally more positive. The stiffening of the springs and fitting of wider wheels had improved handling markedly, and the old Powerglide automatic transmission had been replaced by the greatly superior Turbo Hydra-Matic. Overall finish was infinitely better, but the car now had a harsher ride and the cockpit was still cramped. Even after a revision of the interior that had cost $120,000 and produced an increase in shoulder room of a half inch each side, the Corvette was still, as *Car Life* put it, "... *one heck of a big car for two people and almost no luggage.*" A trunk rack was supplied to increase the car's carrying capacity, but utilizing this reduced rear vision to zero—leaving aside the fact that what was effectively an outside trunk was hardly in keeping with a futuristic automobile. In 1969, the Stingray name was revived—this time as one word instead of two. In spite of all its shortcomings, its noisiness, its harsh ride and its general brutishness, the Corvette was still a very powerful, fast and sexy car.

For '69, the standard wheel width was again increased, from 7 ins. to 8 ins. The small-block engine had had its stroke increased, raising capacity to 350 cu.ins. and was offered in two states of tune, delivering 300 bhp and 350 bhp (one horsepower per cubic inch) respectively. Four versions of the 427 were available. With triple, two-barrel Holley carburetors, a four-speed, Muncie manual gearbox and a 3.55:1 rear axle ratio, a 435 bhp version could accelerate from rest to 60 mph inside six seconds and a standing quarter-mile was possible in fourteen seconds. Crude as the ride quality still was, *Car Life* magazine's comment was no less than the truth: *"... you'd better believe that it takes a lot of car to catch this bear!"*

Bear? Either way, there was even a ZL-1 option, with an all-aluminum block and dry-sump lubrication, developed by McLaren for CanAm racing, that weighed 100 lbs. less than the mighty L-88 option and produced something in the region of 560 bhp. Admittedly, this option increased the price of a "standard" Corvette by some sixty per cent, up from around $5000 to $8000, and only two road-going examples ever left the factory, but it was available for anyone with deep pockets and strong nerves.

Even the small-block Corvettes drew favorable comment now. Only a year after they had considered the new model too tacky to test, *Car & Driver* decided that the car now offered an interesting problem for the prospective purchaser to ponder. *"The small-engine Corvettes are marginally fast and extraordinarily civilized. The large-engine Corvettes are extraordinarily fast and marginally comfortable."* You paid your money and you made your choice. The third shift had raised

output to 38,762—an increase of ten thousand on '68. On November 7, 1969, the 250,000th Corvette came off the line and it looked like the problems were over. In fact, they were just about to begin.

Previous page: The critics criticized but the buyers bought: these two obviously thought it was great! Sales in '68 were up to nearly 29,000.

Left: Sales continued to climb, despite the carping of some, increasing by 10,000 in 1969.

Left Inset: The 350 cu.in. small-block could now deliver one brake horsepower per cubic inch.

Right Inset: Even wth the roof sections removed, the cockpit was still a tight fit for many drivers.

Next Page: In '69 the Stingray name was revived—but this time as one word.

With up to 400+bhp available, a '69 Corvette with a
Muncie 'box could run to 60mph in six seconds and
cover a quarter mile in 14 seconds.

The 'Seventies...

In 1970, an auto workers' union dispute hit production at the St. Louis factory. Whatever the general grievances of the labor force, things can't have been helped by the increased pressure

they were under due to the introduction of the third shift. The net result was a two month delay in the 1970 model reaching dealers' showrooms. This, in turn, led to a massive drop in orders and production slumped to 17,316—the lowest for

Previous page: The '71 Corvette is a rare car, mainly due to labor disputes. The new, LT-1, solid-lifter version of the small-block produced 370bhp. The big block was stroked to 454 cu.ins. and was good for 465 bhp.

The seventies saw the decline and fall of the Muscle Car, but up to '74 there were still some prime examples around, like this '69 Chevrolet Camaro Z-28 (Below), 1970 Ford 302 Boss Mustang (Right Top) and 1974 Pontiac Firebird Trans Am (Right Bottom).

nearly a decade. The '70 Corvette was—and is—therefore a rare car, but unlike a lot of "limited-production" machines, it was—and is—definitely desirable. Despite their troubles, Chevrolet had continued to revise, refine and generally to improve the car. The LT-1 version of the small-block motor was introduced. Utilizing solid lifters, higher-lift cams, more aggressive valve timing and bigger exhaust bore, plus the carburetor set-up from the 427 and cold air intakes, this engine produced 370 bhp @ 6000 rpm. The 350 cu.ins. small-blocks were left unchanged in deference to the Federal emission-control requirements. These were to have an increasingly profound effect upon the burgeoning "Pony Car" market, which was headed by Ford's Shelby Mustangs, Chrysler's Dodge Chargers and GM's Pontiac Firebirds—not to mention Chevrolet's own Camaro Z-28s—all exact contemporaries of the "new" Corvette but none of them exactly sports cars. The big question was how long the Corvette could remain a sports car in the face of increasingly anti-performance-biased government legislation.

The ominous word *luxury* was being bandied around already. Still, in 1970, the 427 had its stroke increased to bring it up to 454 cu.ins. With a 10.25:1 compression ratio, this produced 390 bhp @ 4800 rpm. The aluminum-head LS-7 option ran a compression ratio of 12.25:1 and produced 465 bhp, allowing a standing quarter-mile in around thirteen seconds with a terminal speed of almost 110 mph. The LS-7 was a pure competition engine and none were ever fitted to road cars.

Styling changes were minimal and incremental. The four "gills" cut into the front fenders were replaced by a grille, and this was echoed in the (false) radiator intakes up front. It had been noted that the lower sections of the body were susceptible to damage from stones, thrown up by the wheels. This was addressed by flaring the wheel arches. The twin tail-pipes were changed from round to rectangular. The seats were improved, giving better support and more headroom, and improved access to the luggage area—for there was still no trunk lid. Inertia-reel seat belts were fitted as standard.

Left: 1971 was the last year that horsepower was quoted as a gross figure. The figure for a '71' base 350 engine (270bhp) would, the following year, be shown for the 454.

Right: The price of fresh air...1971 was the year that compression ratios had to be drastically lowered to allow Corvette engines to run on lead-free fuel and thus reduce harmful emissions.

Getting the lead out...

In 1971, GM's president, Ed Cole, decreed that all of the Corporation's automobiles were to be made to run on 91 Octane fuel. This was in response to the approaching Clean Air Bill that would ban the use of lead as an additive in gasoline. Up to this point, engines like the Corvette's big-block, 427 cu.ins. V8 had been intended to run on 103 Octane "Premium" fuel that contained a high level of tetra-ethyl lead as an anti-knock ingredient ("knocking" being pre-ignition). The only way for this reduction in Octane levels could be accommodated was via the drastic lowering of compression ratios—down to levels not seen since the very first Corvette rolled off the line at Flint in 1953. This meant that the small-block V8 now had to run with a compression ratio of 8.5:1, producing a modest 270 bhp @ 4800 rpm. The LT-1 version was cut to 9.0:1, producing 330 bhp @ 5600 rpm. The big-blocks suffered similarly: the LS-5's output fell to 365 bhp @ 4800 rpm and the LS-6's to 425 bhp @ 5600 rpm. The '71 Corvettes were still hardly under-powered. The LS-6 was capable of reaching 60 mph from a standing start in 5.5 seconds, and a standing quarter took it around 14 seconds, reaching 105 mph. Top speed was in excess of 150 mph. Even though some "muscle cars" of the period were now claiming much higher outputs, few, if any, of them could match the Corvette's speed and acceleration—or its handling—on the road.

The versatile T-Top coupe now outsold the convertible Corvette by a ratio of five to three. The fallout from Ralph Nader's infamous 1965 treatise, *Unsafe at Any Speed*, about poor auto design in general—and the inherent, lethal flaws of Chevrolet's 1960 Corvair Monza in particular—was filtering down to auto-makers in the form of ever more draconian directives. The effect of Mr. Nader's writings were profound

Next Page: An auto-workers strike had cut production in half in 1970. Sales of the '71 'Vette crept back up to over 21,000.

Next Page Inset: Attention had been paid to the aerodynamic problems of the Mako II, especially the tendency of its nose to life under acceleration.

and affected all automobile makers including those overseas. Any foreign manufacturer wanting to import cars into the United States would have to ensure that they conformed fully to the relevant Federal and State legislation. The effect of *Unsafe at Any Speed* was global. Initially, there was massive resistance to Mr. Nader's pronouncements, which were seen by some as an assault on personal liberty and by others as a restraint of trade. This resistance eventually broke out into open hostility in the form of "dirty tricks." In March of 1966, James Roche, then president of General Motors, made a public apology to Ralph Nader, admitting that the corporation had paid people to spy on Mr. Nader in an attempt to obtain evidence with which to discredit him.

It seems hard to believe that an attempt to point out the inherent danger of certain automobile designs could have resulted in such behavior, or, indeed, that such designs could have been allowed to proceed to production. The conflict between corporate profit and personal integrity is still with us, but, hopefully, new technologies will ensure that potentially lethal design flaws never get beyond the drawing board or at least the computer display. Whatever: by the beginning of the 'seventies, the days of the all-American convertible were already numbered. There were no styling changes made to the Corvette for 1971, but the new ZR-1 package was offered. This was another pure competition option, comprising the LT-1 small-block engine mated to a heavy-duty, four-speed transmission. The ZR-1 also had an aluminum radiator and carefully revised suspension with stabilizer bars and heavy-duty springs and shock absorbers. Power brakes were fitted as standard but power windows were not an option, along with power steering, air-conditioning, rear-window defroster—or even a radio. Only eight ZR-1s were produced.

Previous Page:
Despite their trials
and tribulations, the
Corvettes of the early
'seventies remain
extremely desirable
automobiles.

Right: Comfort
was now being
emphasized alongside
performance. The
'71 Corvette could still
be called a sports car
but it could hardly be
called spartan.

Performance continued to be de-emphasized. From 1971, horsepower ratings were quoted as SAE (Society of Automotive Engineers) net, a standard that measured "true" output in the sense that it allowed for such mundane, everyday items as air cleaners, pumps and mufflers. Thus LT-1's output was now shown as being down from 350 bhp gross to 255 bhp net. In 1972, the LS-6 option was deleted, leaving the 365 bhp LS-5 as the most powerful 'Vette available. The car's desirability was undiminished, however, and, as if to prove this, the previously optional anti-theft alarm system was now fitted as standard equipment. In an effort to reduce production costs, and so keep showroom prices competitive, Chevrolet was gradually reducing its options lists—in both the cosmetic and the performance departments— across their entire range.

Left: Performance-sapping legislation in the 1970s caused more emphasis on "luxury" features.

Next Page: 1972 saw Corvette performance begin to fall below par.

Crisis? What crisis?

1973 brought with it 5 mph bumpers and the gas crisis. The first was a ruling that all new automobiles had to be fitted with standard-height bumpers that could withstand a 5 mph impact without damage. Many manufacturers achieved this by fitting massive, and spectacularly ugly, cow-catchers in the style of the Volvos then currently a by-word for Scandinavian good sense, if not good taste. The Corvette managed to solve this problem, with considerably more elegance and panache, by fitting deformable plastic body sections front and rear, color-keyed to the car's paintwork. When impacted, by a parking miscalculation or whatever, the "soft" section would simply squash down and return to its correct shape when the pressure was relieved. The only other manufacturer to have employed such a system, at least the only one that springs immediately to mind, is Porsche, in their admirable 928 Series.

The Gas Crisis was an example of mass hysteria fuelled by media sensationalism, but its root cause was serious and has subsequently had far more dramatic and serious consequences. The oil-producing states of the middle-east had banded together to form an association: OPEC (the Organization of Petroleum Exporting Countries) as early as 1960. As a demonstration of their objection to Western support for Israel against its Arab neighbors in the Yom Kippur war of 1973, the OPEC members voted, at their conference in Vienna that year, to increase oil prices by 70%. At a further conference, in Teheran, in December, they agreed to raise prices by a further 130% and a temporary embargo was placed on exports to the United States and to the Netherlands. Prices continued to be increased right though the 'seventies, so that, by 1980, the price of a barrel of crude had risen from $3.00 to $30.00. The massively increased revenues of the OPEC states were invested largely in American

Above: In '73 the Corvette really went soft, with the advent of a deformable nose section, which was colored to match the main bodywork.

and European banks and currency markets. Oil importers looked to other suppliers and/or domestic reserves—Great Britain, notably, drilling in the North Sea. The net result was that demand for OPEC's oil diminished, and with it OPEC's revenues. Conflicts such as the Iran-Iraq war and Iraq's invasion of Kuwait have further undermined OPEC's unity and thus prices and production have both fallen dramatically. Although gasoline prices at the pump never reflected the escalation of OPEC's demands during the 'seventies, the federal government thought it prudent to introduce various measures—many of which seem laughable now—to counter the threat of America's oil supplies running short and having to be rationed. These included the celebrated "Double Nickel" 55 mph speed limit and the fitting of speedometers that read only to 85 mph. Demand for high-performance automobiles slackened considerably and great emphasis was placed on the quest for greater efficiency. In

the short term this spelled the end for the massive, gas-guzzling power plants of the 'fifties and 'sixties. They were like the dinosaurs, powerful and magnificent beasts, but the world had suddenly changed and they were unable to adapt to the new environment and so, sadly, they became extinct. In the long term, the effect of OPEC's price increases and export embargo was entirely positive to the auto industry in general and to the Corvette in particular—but that is still a little way in the future. For the moment, we are still in the era of flared pants and flared wheel-arches...

Left: The '73 still had exposed back bumpers, and optional exposed luggage-carrying facilites.

Left Inset: The tail ights were still round but the tail pipes had become rectangular.

Middle Inset: Bright, fiber-optic exterior light monitors had been deleted from the center console.

Right Inset: Maximum power was now 275bhp (net) from the one remaining 454.

Top: Automatic transmission remained a popular option and seemed appropriate to the gentler, "touring" image that the Corvette was endeavoring to assume.

Right: Radial tires were now standard equipment, but their speed rating was lower than the old bias-belted ones.

The 464 big block V8 had only one more year to run and its output would fall by 5bhp in '74, but loyal devotees still bought Corvettes and '73 sales production was well over 30,000.

It is interesting to compare the Mako Shark II with the '73 Stingray on the next page and the '74 that follows. From the advent of the "soft" tail, the shape of the car would gradually shift away from its forebear's form and towards that of the coming generation.

Below and Next Page:
The '74 got impact-absorbing body panels at the rear as well as the front. The lines of the car were now a lot sleeker than before.

In the climate of the 'seventies, cars like the Corvette were effectively obsolete, although it retained a loyal band of aficionados throughout these troubled times. By 1974, side-impact protection bars had been built into the Corvette's doors and radial tires were fitted as standard equipment. The

lowering of performance that had resulted from de-tuning
for emission control, and the addition of various safety
features, is reflected in the fact that the speed rating of the
radials was lower than that of the old cross-plies.

Previous Page: Magnificent as it is, the 454 cu.in. V8 was a brave choice during the oil embargo of 1974.

Right: The color-coded, impact-absorbing front and rear sections blend perfectly into the '74 Corvette's lines—a stark contrast to the grotesque battering rams fitted to many cars at the time.

Previous Page: There were no exterior changes between '74 and '75 other than the small, rubber pads either side on the license plate—compare this picture with the one preceding it.

Opposite: Mechanical improvements for '75 included electronic ignition and tacho.

Next Page: An endangered species... This 1975 roadster (seen here with its vinyl-covered hard top in place) would be the last of its kind for more than a decade.

Marking time...

Essentially the Corvette's design now remained unchanged. There were no revisions for 1975 at all. Instead, the marketing of the car was revised, gently moving it from being a blood-and-guts road burner to a luxury Grand Touring car. The big-block, 427 V8 was dropped from the options list after a decade. The standard 350 was now de-tuned to deliver a modest (by Corvette standards) 165 bhp whilst the only option remaining was the L-82 small-block, delivering 205 bhp—SAE net, of course. Catalytic converters were fitted in an effort to conform to ever-tightening emission legislation without having to resort to even greater de-tuning. On the plus side... luxury options included electric window lifts, leather upholstery, servo-assisted brakes, air-conditioning and stereo. Maximum speed was around 125 mph and 0–60 mph could be achieved in around 7.5 seconds. Not bad, but hardly the kind of performance that owners had grown accustomed to. It seemed like the Corvette was sliding into comfortable middle-age, putting its feet up and taking things a little easier. This impression was confirmed by the dropping of the convertible body. The roadster had represented the spirit of the Corvette since the original model in 1953, but in July 1975, the last of the line came off the line. Out of a total of 38,465 cars sold in '75, only 4629 were roadsters. It was the end of an era...

The Corvette had become a tradition. It remained unchanged, effectively redundant, and yet had an army of loyal supporters. Despite the fact that the design was becoming increasingly irrelevant, getting heavier and slower and more expensive as every year rolled by (know the feeling?), the Corvette had become a legend in its own long lunchtime. To

demonstrate this, in 1976, the base price broke $10,000 for the first time: the L-48 version of the small-block produced 180 bhp; the L-82 210 bhp; there was no convertible roadster offered; sales increased to 46,558. The following year, with no improvements having been made to the car and the Stingray name abandoned, sales improved again, to a record 49,213.

Beware the Ides of March...

March 15, 1977, saw the 500,000th Corvette come off the line in St. Louis but there would seem to have been little cause for celebration among either the producers or the purchasers. Blind brand loyalty might be sufficient to keep a micro-manufacturer like England's Morgan Motor Company going, with order books full for a decade in advance, but it could hardly be expected to sustain sales figures of 50,000 units a year. Nevertheless, as the same old Corvettes came off the line, the styling basically unchanged from '68 and the performance considerably lower than it had been in '68, there were customers waiting for them. '78 was the silver anniversary of the model; it was twenty-five years since the original, Polo White Corvette was produced, with its Stovebolt Six motor and its two-speed transmission and its ill-fitting side-screens. To mark this occasion, the coupe's styling was finally revised. The upright rear window, set between tapering pillars, was replaced with full, wrap-around glass. Glass roof panels were also available as optional equipment; the car's interior became, instantly, much lighter and brighter than before. All the cars produced in '78 were specially badged and there was a Special Anniversary Edition as well, with a two-tone silver paint job and exclusive aluminum wheels. The engine options remained exactly as before: the 350 cu.ins. small-block in either 185 bhp or 22 bhp tune. Two, four-speed manual gearboxes were available, plus a three-speed, Turbo Hydramatic.

Previous Page: The 1977 Corvette was no longer badged as a Stingray, but production rose inexorably towards 50,000 nonetheless.

Left: '78 was the Corvette's 25th anniversary and all cars got a new, wrap-around rear window.

Right: This 1978 Special Anniversary coupe is "unspoiled." The optional, bolt-on spoilers from the Pace Car replica were incorporated into the front and rear sections for 1980.

Inset: The smart, Special Edition wheels were made of cast aluminum alloy.

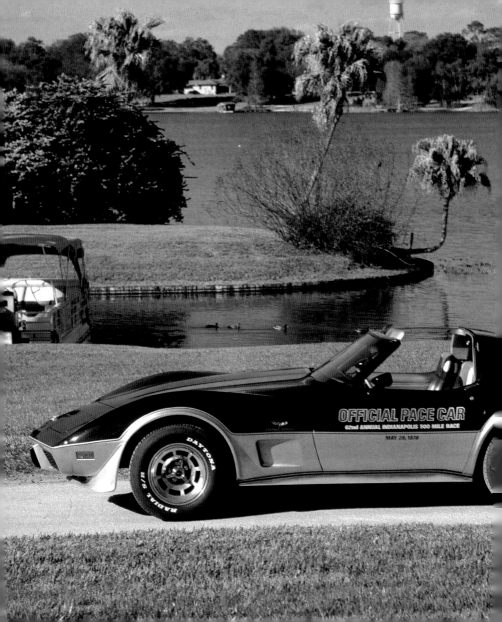

Still setting the pace, sort of...

The other Special Edition for '78 was the Pace Car
Replica. The Corvette had been selected as the
official pace car at the Indianapolis 500 that year
and Chevrolet capitalized on this by producing a
cosmetic copy. The Replica featured bolt-on spoilers
front and rear, plus a two-tone, black and silver paint
job and silver-gray interior trim with lightweight,
leather-trimmed, bucket seats. A set of decals,
identical to those used on the actual Indy pace car,
were supplied, to be applied to the car should the
purchaser so desire. Considering the fact that, in the
case of both the Anniversary Edition and the Pace
Car Replica, the differences from the standard model
were entirely cosmetic, the premium on these models
was considerable: $3,653 on top of the base price of
$10,000. Sales fell, but only slightly, to 47,887. Some
collectors were so eager to get their hands on a Pace
Car Replica that they were bid up to as much a
$6,000 over the already inflated list price.

Left & Next Page: The 1978 Indianapolis Official
Pace Car Replica came with authentic decals
which the owner could choose to have applied
to the bodywork or keep as an investment.

The Pace Car Replica's two-tone black and silver paint job was both striking and attractive. The interior was in silver.

The silver paintwork of the anniversary model
could be combined with a choice of interior
colors. Note the electric window lifts and
mirror adjustment. By 1982, automatic
transmisson would be fitted as standard.

All '78s wore special, Silver Anniversary badges.

The Silver Anniversary Corvette looks more like a luxury tourer than a sports car. This was a very much a sign of the times, and times, as we know, change.

Previous Page: About the only change for '79 was that all cars now came with the improved, lightweight seats from the Pace Car Replica.

Right: 1979 saw sales soar above 50,000 for the first time in the Corvette's history.

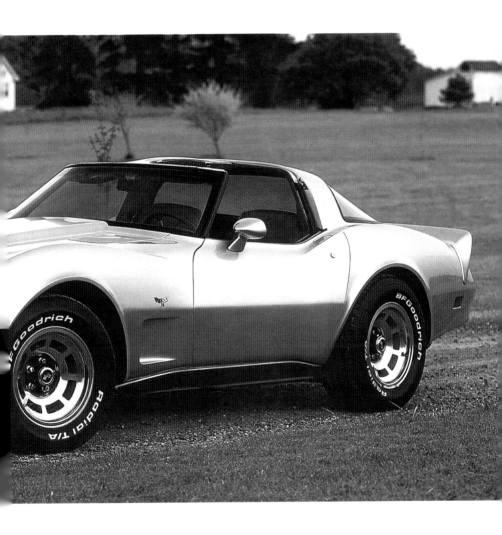

Right: Despite all the complaints that had greeted the new Corvette in '68, sales in 1979 topped 50,000.

The following year the Pace Car Replica's spoilers became an option on all cars and its specially designed, lightweight, bucket seats came as standard. In 1980, the spoilers were incorporated into the deformable front and rear body sections, the marginal improvement in drag coefficient helping to keep down fuel consumption. In a further bid to squeeze more miles per gallon out of the car, attention was paid to weight reduction. The Corvette had been piling on the pounds for over a decade: up from around 3,000 lbs. in '68 to pushing 3,500. In order to reduce this excess avoirdupois, the GRP panels were (literally) slimmed down, as was the glass. Steel, in the front chassis cross-members, differential housing and exhaust manifold, was replaced by aluminum. Kerb weight came down to under 3,200 lbs. The other big reduction was on the dash panel. The 1980 speedo only read to 85 mph, presumably on the assumption that nobody would ever dream of exceeding the newly imposed 55 mph mandatory speed limit by more than thirty miles an hour—even in a Corvette.

Left: Invisible to the naked eye, by 1980, Corvette engneers were making changes, to reduce weight and increase performance.

Next Page: Turbo-charging was in vogue in the early-eighties, and attempts were made to develop a Turbo Corvette.

Although forced induction could provide a bag of additional power, it was heavy on fuel and didn't compliment the silky-smooth power transmission that the Corvette's V8 still delivered.

Next Page: The nose and tail of the 1980 Corvette were neatly reworked to improve aerodynamic efficiency.

Attention to meaningful detail continued, however. In 1981 the rear leaf spring was made in fiber glass, saving some 25 lbs. The one remaining 350 power plant, the L-81, now featured magnesium rocker covers, a stainless-steel exhaust manifold and GM's Computer Command Control engine management system. Output was unchanged but inflation pushed the base price above $15,000—but at least that included a six-way power driver's seat...

The biggest shift to occur with the beginning of the new decade was the transfer of Corvette production from St. Louis to a brand-new, state-of-the-art, dedicated Corvette facility at Bowling Green, Kentucky. The move to Kentucky showed that not only was the Corvette continuing, but that a new model was in the offing. Production had peaked at 53,807 in 1979, but then dropped sharply to 40,614 in 1980. The crazy 55mph speed restriction can't have helped.

Left: Corvette sales had peaked in '79 at 53,807. By '81 they were down to just over 40,606. It seemed almost like the 'Vette was going out of fashion.

Next Page: Integrated spoilers and weight reduction helped to keep fuel consumption as low as possible.

Right & Next Page:
The '81 was fitted
with the L-81 350
small-block, which
incorporated
such features
as magnesium
rocker covers and
stainless-steel
exhaust manifold
and a computer-
controlled engine
management
system.

In the Nick of Time...

The '82 Corvette was intended to be the last of the Mako Shark Generation, and another "Special Edition" was produced to mark the model's fifteen year run. Once again, the outward appearance was unchanged, but for a paint job and some new alloy wheels. This time the pubic wasn't impressed—even by a long-overdue, lift-up rear window that allowed exterior access to the luggage stowage area—especially when they saw the sticker price of $22,537, for less car than they could have had back in 1968 for $4663. Sales collapsed to 25,407, the lowest for a decade. The country was in recession and there was a new energy crisis.

Left: '82 was the last of Mako-generation Corvettes. After fifteen years, the resemblance to the original was still discernible, just.

What hardly anybody had noticed was that, once again, elements of a completely new design were being trailed ahead of time. For the first time since 1965, the 'Vette was a "Fuelie:" the 350 small-block was fitted with a computer-controlled, twin throttle-body "Cross-Fire Injection" system. For the first time since 1955, the 'Vette came with automatic transmission as standard, with no manual option: the new, Turbo Hydra-Matic system was a four-speed, with fuel-efficient lock-up on the torque-converter for all gears save first.

The Corvette was about to re-invent itself, again, but first, an intermission…

Right: The opening rear window was an immensely welcome, long-overdue, innovation. The dropping of the manual transmission option wasn't quite so exciting.

Top: Fuel injection was now back, after a lapse of some sixteen years.

Above: A special Collector Edition interior trim package in tones of silver and gold marked the end of the Mako Shark era.

Right: With its special silver paint scheme, the Collector Edition sold 6,759 copies.

Top: The Collector Edition also had special wheels.

Above: Cross-fire injection sounded very impressive, but by 1982 the cumulative effect of successive government legislation had been to emasculate the power of the engine.

Left: From this angle, the lines of the Mako Shark II can still be made out. The model had lasted, through troubled times, some fifteen years. In 1982, just over 25,000 examples were produced.

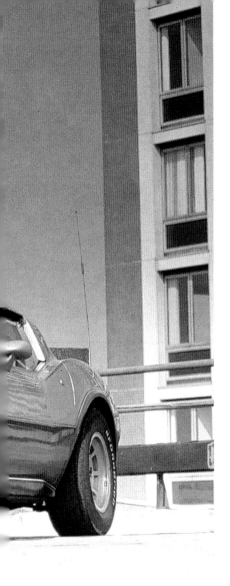

1983

The 1983 Corvette is the rarest automobile on earth. It is more exclusive than the Alfa Romeo 2900B Lungo, more elusive than the Gordon-Keeble, the Facel-Vega or the Isotta-Fraschini, and more evasive than the Maybach. The '83 Corvette makes the Gaylord look like a straight eight, because... there was no 1983. To the Corvette enthusiast, 1983 does not exist. It's like when the calendar was changed from the Julian to the Gregorian system in 1582, and the day after October 4 was October 15. How annoying would that have been if you had tickets for the big game on October 9? If that had happened in 1983, India wouldn't have taken control of the Pujab, the Chinese Communist Party people would have been spared its worst purge since the Cultural Revolution, Lech Walesa wouldn't have received the Nobel Peace Prize, the Baltimore Orioles wouldn't have won the World Series and there would have been no Thirtieth Anniversary Collector's Edition Corvette—which there isn't...

Left: A British-registered,'78 Silver Anniversary Edition. It seems unlikely that the owner will find himself parked next to another one very often.

1984–1996
To Play the King

George Orwell was wrong: 1984 ushered in a Brave, New World!

During the fifteen years of the Mako Generation's reign, another generation had quietly assumed control of the Corvette Family Business. Zora Arkus-Duntov, who had done so much towards transforming the Corvette from a sports car into a Supercar, had retired almost a decade earlier, his place being taken by Dave McLellan. Bill Mitchell put away his pencil in

Below: The '84 Corvette's chassis and body were entirely new and radically improved.

1977, to be replaced at the drawing board by Jerry Palmer, head of the Chevrolet Three Studio. Palmer and McLellan were to form a close partnership, merging form and function fully for the first time. Their departments, working in parallel, would produce a completely new, perfectly integrated package that took into account all of the disparate demands created by the desire for safety, handling, performance, comfort and charisma. Their combined talents produced a car that—like a good coffee or a good scotch—blended smoothness, strength, sophistication and style whilst retaining its own unique identity. Along with GM's director of design, Chuck Jordan, and vice-president of design staff, Irv Rybicki, Palmer and McLennan managed to produce a completely new car that was still, unmistakably, a Corvette. The trail that they followed to reach this happy conclusion, however, traversed a vast area of ground that had been explored previously—and mapped, in detail—by the above-mentioned pioneers.

Below: The family likeness is still visible— the fender vents hark back to the 'fifties—but the '84 design provided an entirely new platform for development.

Top: Even the badge had been revised for '84.

Bottom: The Sixth-generation Corvette had, once again, benefitted from extensive aerodynamic research, resulting in a beautifully smooth profile.

Exploring the alternatives...

The new car's clear, genetic heritage—its "family likeness"—would have been far more difficult to maintain had Chevrolet decided to follow Ford down the mid-engine path. By the late 'sixties, Ford's mid-engined GT40 had established itself as one of the all-time great sports/racing cars, winning at Le Mans for four straight years from 1966 to 1969. Reacting to this, Frank Winchell, then head of Research and Development at Chevrolet, produced an experimental, mid-engined, prototype called the XP-880. This car was shown at the New York Auto Show in 1968 (the same year that the Ford GT40 took the Sports Car Championship) as the Astro II and generated considerable interest. It was at precisely at this time, as mentioned earlier, that Zora Arkus-Duntov had returned from hospital to discover that his position of authority in the Corvette hierarchy had been severely undermined during his absence. Duntov immediately sought to reassert his dominance and produced his own mid-engine design, the 1969 XP-882, which carried the small block V8 mounted transversely behind the passenger compartment, driving the Turbo Hydra-matic transmission via chains with the drive shaft passing through the oil pan—an idea later utilized in the Lamborghini Countach. A couple of prototype chassis were produced and the idea of a mid-engined Corvette began to gather momentum. John DeLorean, taking over as Chevrolet's new general manager, however, soon silenced such discussions by pointing out that such a design would be hugely complex and unfeasibly expensive to develop for volume production.

Heedless of the supposed practical problems, both Duntov and Bill Mitchell had really warmed to the idea of a mid-engined car. Meanwhile, over in Italy, Alejandro De Tomaso, an ex-cattle baron turned race-car driver, whose anti-Peron opinions had forced him to leave his native Argentina, was busily mounting Mustang V8s, centrally, in sinuous bodywork designed by Giorgetto Giugiaro.

The resultant hybrid was named the Mangusta; Mangusta means mongoose and mongooses kill cobras. OK? The combination of Italian styling and American muscle produced a heady cocktail of looks, performance and, crucially, reliability. British Motor Car Distributors in California ordered 200 Mangustas and it became an instant style icon. British Motor Car Distributors was owned by Kjell Qvale, who subsequently acquired Jensen Motors of England and imported the Interceptor III, another magnificent example of successful, trans-Atlantic cross-breeding. In association with Donald Healey, Qvale also produced a small sports car called, naturally enough, the Jensen-Healey. As a young man, Healey had collaborated with George Mason to produce the Nash Healey, one of the very first trans-Atlantics. The Jensen-Healey was fitted with a Lotus developed engine. Although, as we all know, the mid-engined Corvette idea was never brought to fruition, certain parts of this complex story became intrinsic elements in the development of the latest generation of cars.

Anyhow, Ford bought a controlling interest in De Tomaso, along with their subsidiaries: the Ghia styling studio, where Giugiaro had worked, and that of Vignale. The next model produced was the Pantera, which featured a Ford 351-C, 310bhp V8, mid-mounted in a unitary body, styled by Tom Tjaarda, Ghia's American designer, and engineered by Gianpaolo Dallara, who had created Lamborghini's stunning Muira. When this fabulous beast began to appear in Lincoln-Mercury showrooms, along with predictions of 10,000 a year being produced, Chevrolet's XP-882 was hastily dusted off. This time around, Bill Mitchell was charged with the task of styling a version around a four-rotor Wankel engine. With the Ford/De Tomaso marriage in mind, DeLorean hired Pininfarina to style a two-rotor version as

Above: The difference between the '82 and '84 Corvette is subtle.

Opposite Insets: Familiar features included the concealed headlights and the fender vents.

well. Both versions were shown to the public in 1973, to be shelved immediately due to the oil crisis. Even then, and with the departure of Mitchell and Duntov, the idea just wouldn't go away. A prototype named the Aerovette, with a mid-mounted, Wankel engine, was produced in 1977. Even though its name conjured up visions of Eastern-European airlines, the Aerovette was a striking design and it was widely believed that the 1980s would herald the arrival of an all-new, mid-engined Supercar.

In the final analysis, the question of whether the driver ought to sit in front of the engine or behind was settled by… the driver. Whereas Europeans are apparently happy put up with temperamental machinery on the grounds that chronic unreliability is somehow a sign of sophistication, the American motorist is primarily interested in having a car that will start in the morning without having to have the oil warmed in a pan, and which doesn't need re-tuning every week. The Corvette sells throughout the United States, from Alaska's cold to the Everglades. It's a performance car but it must perform at all times and in all places, regardless of heat, cold, rain, snow or relative humidity. American drivers like to be able to get in and out of a car without having to take a course in Yoga and to able to hear the stereo, or even the passenger, above the induction roar. The Corvette works. It's worked since 1953. If it works, don't fix it.

So… 1984 saw the release of a new Corvette that was reassuringly the same and excitingly different. The styling, compared to previous incarnations, especially its immediate predecessor, was remarkably restrained. Signature features—the fold-away headlights and the four, big, round, recessed tail lights—were there, as were the wrap-around rear window from the later Makos and the front fender vents that harked right back to the indented coves of the '56 reworking. The line was now much smoother and less aggressive but still purposeful muscular.

Less is More...

The car was smaller on the outside—nearly 2 inches shorter in the wheelbase (down from 98 inches to 96.2)—and almost 9 inches overall, but due to the abandonment of the Mako's "wasp waist" it was bigger on the inside, with 6½ inches more shoulder room. It was also just over an inch lower. Once again, extensive wind-tunnel testing had helped produce a shape that was not only easy on the eye but also effective through the air, with a drag coefficient of 0.34. This was a 23.7% improvement over the previous body. That meant that, whereas the '79 Corvette required 143 bhp to propel it at 130 mph on level ground in still air, the Palmer body needed a mere 74 bhp. The T-Roof was superseded by a return to a full "Targa" style design, with a one-piece, removable center panel.

A "rubbing strip" ran right around the car's beltline, serving a triple function: it was decorative; it gave some protection to the paintwork against other people's doors being opened against it, or its doors being opened against other people's paintwork, and it concealed the join between the upper and lower body sections. The whole front section of the body hinged forward for engine access —a vast improvement on earlier models—and what it revealed when opened was as impressive as the coachwork. The engine block and fan casing were painted black, the air cleaner was in die-cast magnesium alloy, the battery was custom-produced in black and silver, the HT leads were custom colored—even the dipstick handles were specially designed. Much of the detail design for the new car was the work of a junior member of the Studio Three team, John Cafaro. The styling of the Corvette now extended to the wiring; it was an exercise in attention to detail not seen since the days of the Cadillac V16s.

Left: The remarkable efficient aerodynamics of the new body shape can be clearly seen in this wind-tunnel shot. Drag was reduced by an incredible 23.7%, making the car more fuel efficient before the motor was even started.

4+3 = 22.5

The motor was the "Cross-Fire Injection" computer-controlled version of the 350 cu.in. small-block V8 that had been fitted to the '82 Makos, delivering 205 bhp @ 4300 rpm. Final drive was via either a wide-ratio Turbo Hydra-matic, featuring a lock-up on the torque converter in the top three gears, as seen on earlier models or, alternatively, a complex "4+3" manual developed from the Borg-Warner T-10 unit.

The idea of the "4+3" system was to evade the "Gas-Guzzler" tax loading imposed by the Environmental Protection Agency on cars that failed to return an average 22.5 mpg under simulated "average" driving conditions. Designed by Doug Nash Engineering, of Franklin, Tennessee, the system incorporated a secondary set of planetary gears fixed to the rear of the standard transmission to provide overdrive ratios on second, third and fourth gears. British Triumph TR and Austin Healey sports cars, the Volvo P1800, and others, had used a similar, manually operated, system, manufactured by the impressively-named Laycock de Normanville, mainly during the 'sixties. The Doug Nash, computer-controlled system could be over-ridden by hard acceleration or switched off altogether, but when in use it—not the driver—would determine when to engage the overdrive ratios according to throttle opening, road speed and gear selection. This drove through a standard final-drive ratio of 3.07:1, with a 3.33:1 offered as an option. The Doug Nash system may have pleased the EPA but a lot of customers remained unimpressed and ordered the optional, four-speed, automatic 'box instead.

The Backbone of the Design.

The most innovative and advanced element of the new design was Dave McLellan's chassis design, which benefited from the experimental, mid-engined cars and mirrored the thinking of Englishman Colin Chapman in the small, but perfectly formed, Lotus Elan, which also had fiberglass bodywork. Duntov's ladder-frame, which had served the Corvette admirably since the first Sting Ray, in 1963, was now replaced with a single, aluminum C-section beam that ran through the center of the car connecting the front and rear axles. Over this was placed a one-piece, robot-welded "uniframe" to which the fiber glass body panels were bonded. This chassis, together with the extensive use of weight-saving materials in areas that included the front and rear suspension control arms, the A/C compressor, the brake master cylinder, the mounts for the power steering and the alternator, the transmission casing, the drive shaft and the radiator fan, reduced the kerb weight of the new car from 3232 lbs. to 3087 lbs. The front suspension monoleaf was now fabricated, like the rear's, in glass-reinforced plastic.

The lack of cross-members in the chassis frame enabled Palmer to achieve a lower roof-line without any loss of headroom. By passing the exhaust system, with its attendant catalytic converters, along the broad, central tunnel that carried the drive shaft between the massively improved seats—with optional power adjustment that included lumbar support—he brought the floor of the passenger compartment down to ground clearance level. The hood line was also lower, this being achieved by deleting the carburetor option in favor of fuel injection as standard, seating the engine fractionally lower and locating the

Below: All '84s might have looked like this. Corvette designers had explored the potential of a mid-engined design and they would continue to do so, producing amazing cars like the IMSA GTP.

steering rack (recirculating balls begone!) forward of it. The new, long-awaited, rack and pinion steering was power-assisted, with a ratio of 15.5:1 in standard form and 13:1 in the Z51 Competition Package, which also included "gymkhana" suspension that was stiffened to the point that it was too harsh for normal road use but would permit the car to corner carrying a lateral force of 0.95g, the highest ever recorded by an American production car and higher than a whole lot of European exotics.

Contact with the road was maintained via 15-inch road wheels, 8.5 ins. wide at the front and 9.5 ins. at the rear. These were made in cast alloy and, due to their integral cooling vents for the all-round disc brakes, were non-interchangeable, either left to right or front to rear. 16-inch wheels became available later in the year and a get-you-home-slowly spare was supplied. P255/50 Goodyear Eagle tires bearing uni-directional "gatorback" tread were produced especially for the car.

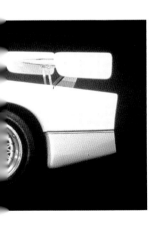

Not surprisingly, the new model was extremely well received by both press and public. The Corvette was once again a match for any foreign sports car. The complex and unpredictable Doug Nash 4+3 gearbox attracted a fair amount of criticism, as did the futuristic dash panel, featuring digital readouts that could well have been inspired by Star Wars. In deep space they might have been effective but in daylight they became illegible. The only other drawback was a base price of $23,360...

Top speed was measured by *Car & Driver* at 140 mph. Sixty miles an hour came up in 6.7 seconds from a standing start and a quarter of mile could be covered, from rest, in 15.2 seconds with a terminal speed of 90 mph. These figures confirmed the fact that the new Corvette was "...*one of the half-dozen fastest production automobiles in the world.*" For the first time since 1979, sales exceeded fifty thousand units, totaling 51,547.

Below: British sports car design influenced the '84 Corvette, as it had the '53. Some lucky Brits even got to own one, usually via dealers Claremont Corvette of Kent.

The Shape of Things to Come...

The outward aspect of the Corvette was now established and would carry the model through to its fortieth anniversary in 1993 and on to its fiftieth in 2003, allowing for a thousand incremental revisions, refinements and improvements. As formerly, the development of the car had been leap-frogged:

the all-new body concealed the true and trusty 350 cu.in. small-block V8, with its cast-iron block and its push-rod & rocker operated valve-gear. This engine was the same one, with the same bore and stroke (4.00 × 3.48 inches), that had graced the line since 1969 and was, even then, merely a stroked version of the 327 that dated from '62. A new motor seemed long overdue, but the performance limitations imposed by strict emission control laws and fuel economy targets had effectively postponed the pressing need for an all-new power plant for more than a decade. Now, however, the new "backbone" chassis and sophisticated suspension layout were obviously capable of handling a lot more power. The question was how would that power be produced. Federal edicts had by this time become a part of the automotive landscape and a return to the glory days of the 427 was as likely in 1985 as a return to detachable side-curtains. It was in 1985, however, that the decision was taken to proceed with a fundamental reworking of the thirty-year old V8. That reworking—the ZR1—turned out to be a lot more fundamental than anyone had at first imagined.

It was decided that the revised engine must be capable of returning the same fuel economy as the L98 but would be aimed at the performance levels of Ferrari, Aston Martin and Porsche. In the words of Chevrolet chief engineer Fred Schaafsma, the ZR1 Corvette was to be "… the best performing production car in the world." The first, somewhat tentative, step along this road was the provision of "Tuned Port" fuel injection, in place of the "Cross-Fire" system, in 1985. This increased output by a respectable, but hardly earth-shattering, 25 bhp. The harsh ride was mollified by a reduction in the spring rates and gas-pressurized shock-absorbers were added. An oil cooler was fitted as standard.

Previous Page: The stiffness of the backbone chassis allowed a return to an unbraced open space when the coupe's roof panel was removed.

Above: The digital instrumentation was a cause of much criticism, a greatly exaggerated flaw in a generally excellent design.

Right: The fabulous IMSA GTP cars could reach speeds well in excess of 200mph with their 1200bhp, turbocharged Chevrolet engines. One of their most notorious outings was at Riverside in 1986, when Doc Bundy managed to test one to the limit—and beyond.

Left: Revisions for 1985 included an oil cooler and revised suspension settings with gas-filled shock-absorbers.

Above: "Cross-Fire" injection was replaced by the "Tuned Port" set-up and increasing compression, releasing an additional 25bhp. Brakes were now anti-lock; cylinder heads were aluminum; roadholding amazing.

The Roadster Returns...

The big surprise for 1986 was the return of a full convertible Corvette, absent since 1975. A true, open cockpit, version of the new body had been anticipated in the basic design and all that was necessary to provide additional stiffness was a chassis cross-member and a lateral beam behind the seats. By happy chance the new convertible was selected as the Official Pace Car for the 70th Indianapolis 500. The actual pace car was finished in bright yellow, but the replica decals could be supplied with any color, so any '86 Corvette convertible was a Pace Car Replica.

Overall improvements included the fitting of anti-lock brakes (ABS) from Bosch. This system was a considerable technological advance, comparable to the introduction of the disc brake. ABS represented a major safety feature, particularly when fitted to a car like the Corvette. For all its good road manners, the car could still deceive an unwary or inexperienced driver with its turn of speed and incredible cornering ability. Power output remained steady at 230bhp but that was more than enough for many, bearing in mind the Corvette's lightweight, fiber glass bodywork and aluminum chassis. With the kind of power increases that the designers had in mind, the world's best brakes would become a necessity rather than a luxury. '86 also saw the introduction of aluminum cylinder heads, a dual exhaust system and the compression raised from 9.0:1 to 9.5:1.

Left: 1986 heralded the welcome return of a genuine rag-top Corvette, seen here in Pace Car Yellow.

Opposite: The
swooping lines of the
Sixth Generation
Corvette were
perhaps even more
effective when the
roof was removed.

General Depression...

"*Chevrolet has the capability of producing something as good
or better than anyone else in the world.*" This was the confident
prediction of ZR1 development manager Doug Robinson, at a
time when the division, and General Motors as a whole, was
going through one of the most traumatic periods in its history.
1986 saw the departure from the GM board of the outspoken,
self-made billionaire H. Ross Perot. Perot famously remarked
that endeavoring to improve efficiency at General Motors was
"*...like teaching an elephant to tap-dance.*" This was acid but
accurate, for the world's greatest auto manufacturer had been
losing its way over the past twenty years, becoming a plodding
pursuer rather than the pace-setter that it had been. In short,
GM's great leadership had slowly been replaced by mediocre
management. Imagination and creativity were frowned upon
and decisions deferred increasingly to the bean counters. The
result, inevitably, was a succession of automobiles so uninspired
and uninspiring that it's a wonder that the shade of Harley Earl
never rose up to smite the evil-doers. Poor products lead to
poor profits as inevitably as night follows day, and The
General's income slumped. Perot, with all his innate diplomacy,
commented on the management style of then GM president,
Roger B. Smith, in a *Newsweek* article, "*Since Roger's been
chairman they've spent over forty billion dollars in capital
improvements, only to lose market share. With the same money,
you could have bought Toyota and Nissan and doubled market
share. That shows you how big forty billion is...*" Considering
the fact that Mr. Smith had, in all fairness to him, used a
considerable chunk of that forty billion to fund the
development of computer-controlled production systems,
including the wholesale purchase of Electronic Data Systems
Inc. (proprietor: H. Ross Perot), this must have been a bitter pill

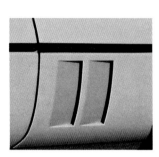

Left: The '84 design had been envisaged as an open car from the outset, so stiffening the frame to produce the roadster was straightforward: an X-member below the floorpan, as in '53!

Above: Detailing was as simple and functional as the overall line of the car. The sum of the parts was one sensational automobile.

to swallow. The GM board decided to invest a further three quarters of a billion dollars, wisely, by using it to pay off Mr. Perot in the most dramatic, auto-industry bust-up since Henry Ford II ousted Lee Iacocca in 1978.

GM laid off almost 30,000 workers and a quarter of its white collar staff. A whole lot of innovative plans and proposals were either cut back or scrapped altogether: production of the potentially highly-competitive Saturn line was reduced by half and plans for GRP bodied versions of the Chevrolet Camaro and Pontiac Firebird were abandoned. The final indignity came when Ford, with only half of GM's automobile sales, showed a greater profit for the first time since 1924.

The 350 cu.ins. small-block V8 was now designated the L-98 and produced 230bhp. Numerous attempts were made to up-grade this engine, via forced induction and multi-valve heads, but it proved pretty much unimprovable.

Always look on the bright side...

In the midst of this doom and gloom, the Corvette team stuck
to their principals and followed their own agenda. In their
quest for the Holy Grail of high performance combined with
low fuel consumption, some seventeen experimental prototypes
came and went. A V6 engine with massively forced turbo-
induction could produce a lot of power, but in a manner far
too uneven for a driver familiar with the turbine-smooth power
delivery of a meaty V8. Twin-turbos were tried on the 350,
but the increase in fuel consumption was unacceptable, the
Corvette driver had to have his cake and eat it! As previously
described, Wankel rotors and mid-engine layouts had already
been weighed in the balance and found wanting. The search

would continue, and the searchers would be aided by friends from a distant land, a land where they drive on the wrong side of the road...

At this time Oldsmobile was developing their Quad 4 engine. This was a four cylinder, with four valves per cylinder, operated by two overhead camshafts, to be offered as an option in their base-range Firenza. Using this design, they

eventually managed to extract nearly 200 bhp from 138 cu.ins. Olds fans who remembered the old days would have recoiled in horror, no doubt, at this heretical adaptation of the mystical digits 4-4-2, but regardless of that, the Quad 4 showed that the multi-valve head was the way ahead, and this, indeed, was the path that the ZR1 design team had decided to follow.

Above: The Corvette's trademark twin tail-lamps remain to this day, having been introduced in 1961.

Left: The new backbone chassis design left a whole lot more room for the occupants than previously

Next Page: By 1986, performance was starting to become more exhilarating; 0 to 60 now took around six seconds. The Corvette was feeling frisky again.

Hands across the Sea

1986 had seen the acquisition by GM of a controlling interest in the miniscule British manufacturer of miniscule British sports cars, Lotus. Lotus had built up an enviable reputation in Formula One Grand Prix racing and had also produced some truly great automobiles. The Elan, for instance, featured a fiber glass body, mounted on to a backbone chassis. The Jensen-Healey, mentioned earlier, had a Lotus-developed, twin-cam, sixteen valve engine that was fitted tipped over at an angle to allow for a low bonnet line. Tony Rudd, Lotus's technical director, had entered into an agreement with GM, about a year before the takeover, to design twin-cam, sixteen-valve cylinder heads for the L98. The main problem for Mr. Rudd and his team was that it was a *sine qua non* that the new engine should be able to fit between the chassis side rails when installed from below on the Bowling Green line. In one of those strange twists of fate, just as it had been the British sports cars of the 'forties and 'fifties that had inspired the styling of the original Corvette, so a British sports car manufacturer would supply the inspiration for the engineering of its latest—and undoubtedly greatest—incarnation, fifty years on.

While the gentlemen of England wrestled with the problem of trying to get more motor into the same space, whilst retaining the existing bonnet line height, the Corvette continued to gain power and refinement back home. 1987 heralded the introduction of roller valve lifters that reduced

Left: 17-inch wheels, wearing huge Goodyear Eagle tires, were available on the '88. After 35 years, output was close to 900,000 cars.

Left: Access to the engine and its ancillaries was superb, which must have greatly aided those who sought to obtain maximum performance from the L98 for competition purposes.

friction and increased output by ten horsepower to 240bhp. An optional tire-pressure monitor was offered, which signaled a drop in pressure of one pound per square inch on any wheel, via a dash panel display, to the driver. Also available—at considerable extra cost—was a Twin-Turbo conversion produced by Callaway Engineering. This boosted output to 345 bhp and came as part of a competition package that enabled the car to achieve 175 mph top speed and hit sixty from rest in under five seconds.

By this time, having exhausted every avenue of research in their attempts to re-invent the venerable L89, including chain-driven cams mounted at an angle to the cylinder block (tipped into the V to reduce height), Tony Rudd had come back to Dave McLellan with the conclusion that the only way to achieve what was required was to start from scratch. He'd made his point and the decision was made to produce what was to become known as the LT5 engine.

Drivers like Stu Haynes continue to take the Corvette to the track and come home with trophies, as they did back in 1988, for Tom Bell, and more recently on behalf of Trenton Forging.

Chevrolet dealer Tom Bell, of Redlands, California, has been involved with Corvette racing for more years than he probably wants to be reminded of. These pictures show that, although fully prepared for the rigors of competition, the car is, underneath, like the ones in Mr. Bell's showroom.

Previous Page: Brakes were beefed up for '88 and the suspension was modified to prevent rear-end squat under acceleration.

Previous Page Inset: The cockpit display remained pure *Star Wars* and probably appealed to many for that reason.

Right: The 1988, monochrome, 35th Anniversary Edition trim package was limited to 2000 copies for sale, plus another 50 for show.

Next Page: The Anniversary Edition featured white seats and steering wheel plus a tinted glass roof panel. Luxury equipment included air-conditioning, electric seats and mirrors and a Delco/Bose stereo system. Output was up to 245bhp.

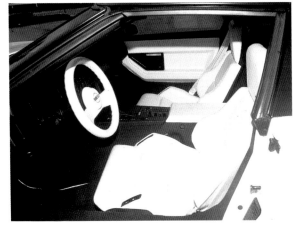

The 35th Anniversary edition naturally included exclusive badging. Sadly, sales had slipped to under 23,000 cars in total as the base price nudged $30,000.

As work on the new engine progressed through 1988, the L89's output rose to 245 bhp, courtesy of a reworked exhaust system and re-profiled cams. The suspension was also revised and larger and thicker brake discs utilizing dual-piston front calipers, were fitted to redesigned, alloy wheels with an optional diameter of seventeen inches. These were shod with immense P275/40ZR Goodyear Eagle tires.

As no cars were officially produced in 1983, the Corvette's thirtieth birthday had passed unmarked. '88 was the thirty-fifth year of production and a limited edition anniversary model (RPO Z01) was offered. 2050 coupes were built, finished in white with black detailing and a tinted glass roof panel. The interior was white leather trimmed and equipped with climate control, power seats and door mirrors, heated rear window and a Bose stereo system. Output for '88 was 22,789 cars. Total production had reached almost 900,000.

The white bodywork and black roof details of the '88 anniversary model recalled the original, any-color-so-long-as-it's-white roadster that rolled proudly off the Flint production line at the end of June, 1953.

Previous Page: The Corvette Indy was first shown at the Detroit Automobile Show in 1986 and demonstrated how dedicated Chevrolet were to "mid-engined Corvette research and image studies."

Right:
The Indy featured a monocoque design and was constructed largely from Kevlar and carbon-fiber. The detachable canopy was formed from cast acrylic material. Door opening is a la Countach.

Right: Fly-by-Wire...
The Indy features
four-wheel drive and
four-wheel steering,
both controlled
electronically. Its
twin-turbo, Ilmore-
Chevrolet, Indy Car
V8 was modified to
run on standard
gasoline.

Right: Whilst Lotus were working on on the LT5 in England, Reeves Callaway, in Old Lyme Connecticut, was managing to extract over 380bhp from the pushrod L98 via the use of twin Rotomaster turbochargers. Note the intercooler vents cut into the hood of this 1989 example of his work..

Below: The ZF 6-Speed was a welcome relief from the complex CAGS 4+3 system.

Skip the details...

In 1989, tantalizing glimpses of the ZR1 appeared ahead of the rest of it. The first of these took the form of a six-speed, manual gearbox designed jointly by Chevrolet and the highly respected Zahnradfabrik Friedrichshafen AG, (ZF), of Germany. This was a massive improvement on the never-popular Doug Nash 4+3, though it incorporated a feature that was to prove controversial, to say the least. As part of the effort to keep fuel consumption out of the "gas-guzzler" league, a system, officially named Computer Aided Gear Selection (CAGS), but also known as the "skip-shift" was employed. On light throttle openings (below 35%) and at speeds of between twelve and nineteen miles per hour, when the driver

Opposite & Below:
Corvettes undergo
the final inspection at
Bowling Green. Every
detail: mechanical,
electrical, interior, and
exterior is thoroughly
scrutinized before the
cars are dispatched.

moves to change up from bottom gear the system will lock out second and direct the shift lever across the gate into fourth. This feature, which, in the hands of (and under the right foot of) a dedicated Corvette driver, might never be activated, and combined with a monumentally tall sixth gear for highway cruising, would help to keep the Corvette out of the EPA's bad books. This was despite the fact that it was used in conjunction with the LT5 engine that was just about to turn the Corvette world on its head—or put it back on its feet, depending on how you look at it.

Another whisper on the breeze was RPO FX3 (Selective Ride Control). This was available only on cars fitted with the six-speed gearbox and the Z51 handling package. Developed by GM's Delco division, in association with Bilstein, the SRC system used microprocessors to activate miniature electric motors at the top of each shock absorber. These, in turn, operated rotary valves that controlled the flow of fluid into the piston. The system monitored and adjusted itself ten times per second and functioned during compression as well as during rebound. The driver is offered a choice of settings (*Tour—Sport—Perf*) to suit his mood

35TH ANNIVERSARY

CORVETTE
THE REAL THOROUGHBRED

and the driving conditions. Within each setting the damping rate increases with the car's speed in six, twenty-five-mile-per-hour steps, from 25mph to 150mph. Such is the sophistication of the system, and so much thought has gone into its application, that the speeds at which damping is reduced are set five miles per hour slower to avoid the car constantly shifting between settings while cruising at one of the above speeds. Set to *Touring*, the suspension will partially absorb ruts and pot-holes on back roads, while the *Performance* setting effectively transforms the set-up to that of a race car. With the level of performance that SRC was trailing, the ride could never be sufficiently "soft" for limousine comfort, but the system assured that it need be no harder than was absolutely necessary for safety. The base L98 equipped Corvette now retailed at $31,545.

King of The Hill

The sixth-series Corvette had started out as a very good car and had got progressively better. The advent of the ZR1, effectively the seventh series, was to make it into one of the all-time greats. At a cost of somewhere in the region of twenty-five million dollars, Dave McLellan and Tony Rudd achieved the near-impossible in engineering terms. Their goal had been an engine that would produce around 400bhp and 400ft. lbs. of torque, run smoothly at idle, be docile at low speeds, be capable of (extremely) high speeds and scorching acceleration, but not consume excessive quantities of fuel in the process. The result of their massive investment of time, talent and money was the LT5.

Right: Anatomy of a masterpiece: a full cutaway of the legendary ZR1

Opposite Inset: The Kingmaker: Dave McLallan, worthy successor to Ed Cole and Zora Arkus-Duntov.

The engine measures 26.6 × 28.2 × 26.5 inches (11 cubic feet), including its hefty emission control system, allowing it to be fitted into the same space as the L98 unit. Its displacement is exactly the same: 350 cu.ins. Output was originally quoted at 375bhp @ 6200rpm, torque at 375ft. lbs. @ 4200rpm. The engine met all US federal emission fuel consumption standards and was able to deliver power smoothly throughout its range, from 650rpm to 7200rpm.

The block was cast in aluminum alloy, with "wet" cylinder liners that were hardened with a Nikasil (nickel and silicone) coating. The liners were machined on both inner and outer surfaces to help with heat dissipation. Due to the increased thickness of the cylinder walls, it was necessary to extend the piston stroke (from 3.48 to 3.66ins.) in order to keep the overall dimensions within the limits dictated by the space between the chassis side-rails.

The resultant, slightly over square bore/stroke ratio placed considerable stresses on the crankshaft, whose design presented one of the trickiest problems for Rudd and his team to solve and it took them over a year to do so. Chevrolet had initially advocated the employment of an iron crankshaft but in practice this proved to be prone to flex and, under extreme conditions, to failure. Production engines were therefore fitted with nitrified forged steel crankshafts and connecting rods. The crankshaft was drilled to aid internal lubrication and runs in five oversize main bearings. The crank cradle is formed from a single, aluminum casting which is bolted to the block. The aluminum crankcase is in two sections and the block itself is extensively ribbed and gusseted for maximum strength.

Opposite: Note that the ZR1 is badged LT5, denoting its very special power plant.

Below Left: Every LT5 motor was individually bench run at Mercury Marine before dispatch to Bowling Green for installation.

Below Right: On the road—375bhp plus...

The four camshafts are driven from the crank shaft via a silent, inverted-tooth primary chain between the crank and an idler, which halves the revolutions. A pair of duplex chains with tensioners then transmit drive to the camshaft sprockets. The valves are operated directly by the cam lobes and employ hydraulic bucket tappets to reduce and simplify maintenance. Space limitation dictated a narrow (22°) angle between the valves; the camshaft bearings and covers are cast as a single piece.

For the sake of compactness, the starter motor, ignition coils and A/C compressor are tucked into the V of the cylinder head and other accessories are fitted to cast engine mountings rather than using brackets. The oil pump is driven from the center of the crankshaft, but the water pump, steering pump, A/C compressor and alternator all share a single drive belt.

Left and Above: Perfect and practical in all its parts, the Corvette ZR1 was one of the most potent pieces of machinery ever to grace a highway.

1988 GRP Corvette bodies process down the Bowling Green line (main picture) to be bonded to their aluminum frames (right). When the engine, transmission and running gear have been installed, each car is checked individually on the rolling road (below).

The Nature of the Beast

The LT5 blocks were produced in Texas, the sump came from Missouri and the head from England, together with the crankshaft and con-rods. The pistons and cylinder liners were made by the German company, Mahle. Finally, the engines were assembled by Mercury Marine of Stillwater, Oklahoma. Mercury was chosen for its familiarity with lightweight, high-revving speed-boat motors.

The bodywork was stock Corvette at the front, but the rear portion was widened to accommodate the massive wheels and tires necessary to transmit the ZR1's prodigious power. The tail was three inches wider than a standard 'Vette and there was nearly six inches more rubber on the road. The rear panel was rounded off more than on the standard car, but the four, signature Corvette tail lamps were squared up! The round, dual tail pipes were replaced by a pair of twin, rectangular tail pipes. It made sense that the main distinguishing features of the ZR1 were put at the back of the car, because that was the part that most other drivers would get to see most often. From the front, probably the only giveaway was the purple-tinted "Koolof" windshield. This was designed to reflect sunlight and thus keep the interior cool, but the fact that it was effectively impervious to infra-red made the use of a dash-panel-mounted radar detector impossible. This little problem was solved on production models by leaving a small, untinted "window" section at the bottom of the screen—for a remote device to open the garage door, obviously.

Left: The ZR1's "Valet Key"allowed the owner to convert the character of the car from *Lassie* to the *Hound of the Baskervilles* at will.

Inside, a colorful, if confusing, "aircraft-inspired" digital instrument panel delivered a mass of largely illegible and irrelevant information to a driver who, if he was using his car as nature intended, wouldn't be looking at it anyhow. Similarly, the switchgear was strewn about the cockpit with reckless abandon. None of this would have worried those fortunate enough to be able to purchase one of these fabulous machines, as the driving experience eclipsed all other considerations. A second ignition key, known as the "valet key," enabled the owner to restrict the engine's output to a mere 240bhp. This was achieved by closing off the larger of the two inlet valves to each cylinder, and shutting down one of the injectors. The idea of this device was to limit the exploitation of the engine's full potential to those whom the owner deemed worthy, i.e. to the owner...

Below Left: The mighty LT5—32 valves, sixteen injectors, 380bhp and 375 lb.ft. of torque.

Below Right: Top speed, in fifth gear, was over 175mph. Sixth gave 42mph for every 1000rpm.

Opposite Left: Familiar flip-up lights

Opposite Right: Interior fittings and controls recall airplane design. Misterearl would surely approve.

When this restriction was removed, a dashboard indicator announced Full Engine Power and the entertainment could truly begin. The ZR1 was capable of sprinting from rest to 60mph in 4.5 seconds. This phenomenal progress continued, undiminished, until beyond the 130mph mark, at which point drag would begin to reduce the rate of acceleration. The top speed, which was somewhere in the region of 175mph, was achieved in fifth gear. Pushing the motor to the rev limit of 7200, first gear would take the car to 56mph, while sixth (0.50:1) allowed interstate cruising at 42mph per 1000rpm. Were the engine capable of pulling maximum revs in top gear, the theoretical maximum speed of the Corvette would be 302.4mph. Maybe it was for this reason that European export models showed 300 on the speedo... In real terms, the ZR1's performance was equal to that of a Ferrari Testarossa or a

Lamborghini Countach, at well under half the price, and with a 60,000-mile warranty. Tuning could raise engine output to 600bhp, putting a genuine 200mph top speed within reach for competition use. Chevrolet were hopeful of overseas interest in the ZR1, and details like a one-size-fits-all license plate recess reflected this, as did the ability of the instrumentation to convey information in either imperial or metric units (175mph is 280 kilometers per hour!), and the use of separate tail light lenses to allow for the fitting of different colors.

1990 was the first full year of production, a small number of ZR1s having been assembled in '89 for the use of motoring correspondents and road-testers. Offered only in coupe form, 3,049 cars were sold, at a base price of $58,995—making the ZR1 the most expensive Corvette of all time by margin of more than $20,000.

By the end of its brief but distinguished career, the ZR1 had gained analog
instruments to measure the performance of its up-rated LT5, which finally
peaked at 405bhp. The last batch of 448 cars were delivered in 1995.

Right: The ZR1 is surely destined to become one the great collectibles of American Automobile history—the Duesenberg of the post-war era.

Right: From the outside, the 1990 Corvette coupe was indistinguishable from the ZR1, but was less than half the price.

Next Page: 1991 saw the Corvette's lines updated and smoothed out slightly. A "retained power" feature allowed auxilliary systems to function briefly after the ignition had been turned off.

King for a day

1991 saw a minor restyle across the whole of the Corvette range, with a smoother, slightly more rounded treatment of the front end. Many of the features that had been, initially, restricted to the ZR1, found their way into and on to L98 equipped cars, including the rear panel with its distinctive square tail lights. This may have irritated those who had paid a hefty premium for such subtle indicators of exclusivity. Now only the high-level rear brake light and wide tires served to distinguish the King from his loyal subjects. RPO FX3, the Selective Ride Control option, was made available on convertibles and so could be had on any car. Such was the excitement that had greeted the announcement of the ZR1 that some people had bid a hundred thousand dollars to secure one but, to their horror, ZR1 sales in '91 fell back to 2,044—a reduction of a third—and cars were soon being offered at a discount. In fact, total sales fell to 20,729. The ZR1 was now listed as an option package, at $31,683—almost doubling the price of the standard coupe. Within two years of its triumphant launch, the ZR1 was being discounted.

LT1

David R. McLellan handed over the coveted post of Corvette chief engineer to David Hill in September 1992. In a strange parallel to the ZR1, Hill had worked on Cadillac's Allante—another fine car that failed to persuade the public of its merits. At a time when the US economy in general, and General Motors in particular, were having to weather a severe economic storm, it would require courage and determination to steer the Corvette safely through. Despite initial misgivings by some that Dave Hill was not as committed as his predecessor to preserving the Corvette's unique features, he proved more than equal to the task.

The true and trusty small-block V8 was once again reworked, to deliver an additional 55bhp. Renamed the LT1, it

became freer and higher revving, though with a little less torque than it had produced in its L98 incarnation. Output was now up to 300bhp and the zero-to-sixty time down to 5.4 seconds, taking what was supposed to be the "cooking" Corvette well into the King's territory. The LT1 received a rapturous welcome from press and public alike, demonstrating once again the innate faith of the American driver in the eternal verities. Four camshafts and thirty-two valves are fine, so long as there's a suitably qualified mechanic within striking distance, but there's something about a cast iron, push rod V8 that inspires confidence in Mid-Western motorists.

The LT1's compression was up to 10.5:1 even on low-octane gas. This was thanks to the superior cooling abilities of the aluminum cylinder heads, electronic ignition timing that could sense pre-ignition, and reverse-flow cooling. The cooling system was derived from the LT5 engine. Lotus had decided that it would be far more effective to pass the coolant direct from the radiator to the cylinder heads, where it was needed most. This was a reversal of the standard route, which, aided by convection, took the coolant up through the water jackets of the engine block and then allowed it to drop back through the radiator. In order to reverse the flow, a powerful pump was employed, driven directly from the camshaft. The LT1 was the most powerful standard Corvette engine since the heady days of the 'sixties, allowing for the difference in measurement standards, and was also employed, in 275bhp tune, as an option in the Chevrolet Camaro up to 2002. The "Opti-Spark" electronic ignition proved extremely susceptible to damp early on and modifications, particularly to the venting of the system to prevent condensation, had to be undertaken. Overall, however, the improvements far outweighed the problems and the LT1 was a hit.

Top: The Corvette's lines seemed to be cleaner than ever; beneath them, the car was growing ever more sophisticated.

Bottom Left: The cockpit is rendered more elegant by the fact that it is now completely functional.

Bottom Right: The small-block was re-designated LT-1 for '92, gaining 55bhp and extra torque.

Another notable innovation was Anti-Slip Regulation (ASR), a traction-control system developed by Bosch that utilized the ABS sensors on the rear wheels. This detected the onset of wheel spin and simultaneously applied (anti-lock) braking to the offending wheel while retarding the ignition and feathering the throttle—it even pushed the pedal back against the driver's foot to let him know that it was operating. In wet and slippery conditions ASR was a valuable safety feature which allowed the car to be driven significantly faster—truly the best of both worlds—although it could cause significant wear increase on the rear brake pads. The system could be disabled for days at the drag strip or the racetrack. With 375bhp to control, it was especially welcome on the ZR1, but despite this, sales of The King of the Hill continued to descend: '92 ZR1 sales were a mere 502, whereas standard hatchback and convertible sales rose slightly, to 14,102 and 5,875 respectively.

On July 2, 1992, the one millionth Corvette was driven off the Bowling Green assembly line. Like the first car to come off the line at Flint, Michigan, it was a white convertible. It would be perhaps the least-traveled Corvette ever produced, as it was destined for the brand new National Corvette Museum that was being built right across the street—at 350 Corvette Drive. The Museum was built entirely with private funds—though Chevrolet were to be extremely generous with their bequests in terms of exhibits—proof of, and memorial to, the affection that the Corvette had earned in the heart of the American public, both drivers and dreamers.

Forty Years On

Sufficient LT5 engines were assembled at Stillwater in 1993 to allow for 448 cars a year to be sold up to the end of 1995, plus a reserve to be held against warranty claims, after which it was discontinued. The arrival of the Dodge Viper RT/10, with its Lamborghini-engineered, all-aluminum, 488 cu.ins., 395bhp, V10 engine, which had paced the '91 Indianapolis 500—driven by Carol Shelby himself—goaded Chevrolet into increasing the output of the ZR1 to 405bhp. This also served to re-establish the output gap between the LT5 and the LT1. This necessitated a re-working of the heads and the beefing up of the main bearings. Though there was hardly any improvement in acceleration, top speed was boosted to as-near-as-dammit 180mph.

The LT1 cars got new tires, courtesy of Goodyear again, in the form of directional and asymmetric Eagle GS-C. As previously, these were exclusive to the Corvette for their first year of production. The tread pattern was "handed" as before, but now the tread was designed to allow for the different cornering stresses exerted on the inner and outer edges of the tire. The handling was tremendous, but tire

replacement had to be carefully considered, as none was interchangeable with any other. The digital dash was also revised, if not greatly improved. Passive Key Entry (PKE) was introduced, which sensed the proximity of the key fob and unlocked the doors as it approached, or locked them as it receded, tooting the horn to let the carrier of the keys know that all was secure.

The Corvette was now forty years old, but rather than slowing down, it seemed to be just getting into its stride. A metallic, Ruby Red commemorative edition was produced, and accounted for about a third of annual sales. The leather interior was color-coded to the paintwork and adorned with various badges and embroideries. Under the hood, the motor was supplied with sound-deadening, polyester rocker covers.

To cope with the cornering forces that the Corvette was capable of generating, '93 cars were fitted with even more massive wheels and tires: Front rims were now eight and a half inches wide, rears nine and a half.

Right: There's little
to distinguish this '94
Corvette from the
ZR1 on the outside,
except that The King
now had five-spoke
alloy wheels.

The Last of the Few

1994 saw the introduction of
distinctive—and distinguishing—
new five-spoke, alloy wheels on
the ZR1. With production
limited to 448 cars per year—all
of which were sold!—these, plus
the up-rated, 405bhp engine,
made these cars the most
desirable of all, particularly as
the "option" price was reduced
to $31,258. The last cars were
produced over the following
year with the final batch of LT5s
from Mercury Marine.

Maybe it was something to
do with being over forty—the
drivers, not the car—but for '94
the Corvette's seats were gently
widened and their controls
relocated to the center console.
The newly-mandatory,
passenger-side airbag was
located where the glove locker
had been previously, a stowage
compartment being incorporated
in each of the arm rests by way
of compensation. The engine's
computer management system
was re-christened Power train
Control Module (PCM) and
extended its influence to the also

new, electronic automatic transmission option. It was now necessary to depress the brake pedal before the selector could be moved out of Park.

September '94 saw the official opening of the museum, which attracted some two thousand Corvettes, of all ages, from every state of the Union and even from overseas. Chevrolet supplied a number of significant cars, on "permanent loan," for display, including the original Sting Ray and Mako II. Duntov and McLennan both showed up for the festivities and the new management was able to celebrate the fact that sales were up—again—to a total of 23,200. This was in spite of the fact that base prices were now up to record levels; the convertible started at $43,665.

Left: All Corvettes were fitted with the ZR1-style square tail lights from '91.

Right: The '95 'Vette was *so* hot, as the English plate on this one seems to imply. It was also so smooth, as the suspension system had been refined pretty much to the point of pefection.

The '95 Indy 500 was paced, once again, by a Corvette, and this prompted yet another Replica. It was the third time that a Corvette had been granted this singular honor—and not the last. The 527 convertible Pace Car Replicas were finished in Metallic Purple over Arctic White, with white hoods. The usual set of decals, which could be applied by dealers should the purchaser so specify, were supplied, plus embroidered badges on the headrests. The Replica was also graced with the previously exclusive "A-mold" alloy wheels from the ZR1.

A new option to appear in '95 was the GS-C Eagle Extended Mobility Tire (EMT). These had reinforced sidewalls that enabled the tire to run flat for up to two hundred miles, at a maximum speed of

Right: Looking like a shark in a goldfish pond, the '95 Corvette dominates a parking lot full of European compacts.

55mph. Bearing in mind the total non-interchangeability of the rubber on the Corvette, this was a useful innovation and allowed for a weight-saving abandonment of the spare, for those sufficiently confident in the EMT. Road noise was a little higher with the EMT, but it was destined to become standard on all models from 1997. The lockout feature on reverse on 4-speed manuals was deleted, having survived since 1959—another link with the past gone!

The passing of the ZR1 led to the introduction of an even hotter version of the 350 cu.in., cast iron, pushrod, small-block V8. This was the 330bhp LT4, which was only available with manual transmission and was mandatory with the six-speed gearbox. The LT4 was a mere 45bhp short of the output of the original LT5. 1000 "Grand Sport" versions were built, commemorating the racing Sting Rays of 1963. They were finished in Admiral Blue with a white stripe and black, or black and red, interior trim. The wheels were the ZR1's A-molds, sprayed black and fitted within bolt-on flares over the rear wheel arches, which recalled the wasp-waisted Stingray.

The 1996 Sebring Silver Collectors Edition proved hugely popular, briefly ousting Red as the preferred Corvette color. This edition also had the A-mold, five-spoke alloys but was available with either manual or automatic transmission. Various interior colors were offered, adorned with a selection of badges and embroidery.

The competition-inspired Z51 suspension option was reintroduced after a five-year lay-off, and a brand new Real Time Damping (RTD) system was introduced as a replacement for the FX3 option. This was another example of overlapping Corvette technological advance, coming as it did in advance of the new C5 model. The system was incredibly complex, but highly effective and reliable.

Left: With the passing of The King, all Corvettes gained the elegant, spoked wheels that had previously been restricted to the ZR1.

Next Page: The 1996 Collector Edition signalled the end of the sixth generation.

Top: The '96 Collectors Edition special logos and Sebring Silver paint added $1250 dollars to the price sticker.

Left Inset: In standard form, the '96 LTI was 300bhp. The LT-4 version, fitted to the "Grand Sport" was good for 380 bhp @ 5800rpm.

Right Inset: All Corvettes were luxurious by 1996. 6-way power-operated sports seats were optional (standard on the G.S.), trimmed with leather, naturally.

Main: Yet another commemorative edition appeared in '96. Under the paint job, all Corvettes could be equipped with "selective real time damping" for $1695.

1997–2003
Z06: The Best Gets Better

The King is Dead... Long Live the King!

The eagerly awaited C5 series Corvette was launched in January 1997 at both the Detroit and the Los Angeles Auto Shows. A new line was to have been introduced in 1993, but due to the appalling problems that General Motors had been wrestling with in the late eighties and early nineties, development had been delayed and almost abandoned.

As with previous model revisions, the body shape was reworked, but this time an entirely new chassis *and* engine were introduced simultaneously—in fact there was hardly any "carry-over" from the previous series. That said, many features of the now departed ZR1 were to find their into the stock Corvette. This was, naturally, the sleekest and fleetest to date, but it was also the most practical, the most comfortable and the most economical—at least in terms of fuel consumption.

One of the perennial problems that Corvette designers and engineers had tried to address from the earliest days was producing a frame of sufficient strength and stiffness to handle the prodigious power that successive generations had been blessed with, whilst at the same time providing a standard of ride comfort acceptable to a domestic driver. The C5's chassis was based on a pair of extremely light but immensely strong, hydro-formed rails. This design was so stiff that it could support the new Corvette's fiber glass body, even as a full convertible, with the rigidity of a standard steel sedan. The twin rail design, though expensive to put into production, eliminated the torque-flexing and scuttle shake that had plagued some previous models, notably the early, ladder-framed Makos. The effectiveness of this design was demonstrated by the fact that the coupe's Targa top could be clipped into place in seconds, rather than having to be secured with bolts at each corner as a "stressed member" providing additional stiffening to the frame, as was the case with the C4.

Ride quality was enhanced by a substantial increase in the wheelbase—up by eight inches to $104\frac{1}{2}$ inches. This provided a more spacious interior and gave greater stability at speed. The cost of this was a slight loss of steering response, probably only noticeable to those drivers who habitually frequented mountain switchback roads. To the vast majority of owners, it represented a massive improvement in ride quality. It had been noted that the increase in the Corvette's price had been matched by an increase in its purchaser's age. The 'Vette was acknowledged to be no longer for boy-racers...

Structural integrity and weight distribution were retained and improved respectively, by the adoption of a trans-axle drive system for the 4L60E automatic transmission. This placed the gearbox at the rear of the car, just ahead of the back axle. The drive shaft was encased in a "torque tube" and the auto box was given a completely redesigned, aluminum housing. Six-speed, manual transmission was available as an alternative, for an additional $815. The rear-mounting of the transmission "automatically" provided so much additional space in the cockpit footwells that a left foot rest was deemed necessary for the driver.

The engine was still a 350, but cast in aluminum, like the ZR1's LT5, rather than formed from cast iron as was the evergreen L98/LT1. Denominated the LS1, this engine was manufactured in Romulus, Michigan, rather than in Flint, where all previous small-blocks had been assembled. It was

forty-four pounds lighter than the LT1 and 45bhp more powerful. Research had shown that the established firing order, 1-8-4-3-6-5-7-2, could induce fuel starvation from adjacent cylinders firing together. The order was therefore revised to 1-8-7-2-6-5-4-3. This produced an unfamiliar, syncopated rhythm at idle, which some owners found unacceptable and "cured" by fitting a balancer pipe between the dual exhausts. The problems caused by wet conditions and condensation to the LT1's forward mounted distributor were cured by adopting a crankshaft trigger, with a separate coil for each spark plug.

Five-spoke, alloy wheels were fitted as standard, again recalling the ZR1. The fronts were 17 inch x 8 inch and the rears 18 inch x 9 inch; they wore Goodyear EMT (run-flat) tires as standard, which precluded the need to carry a spare. For European markets, however, lightweight magnesium wheels, made by Speedline of Italy, were supplied to conform with local legislation. As with the ZR1 and subsequent models, provision was made for foreign detail variations in areas such as the tail lights, and the license plate mountings. High-intensity rear fog lights could also be provided, for territories where such things were mandatory—Olde London Town, maybe? Indeed, the Corvette was garnering foreign sales as never before—a tribute to the car's international reputation for both performance and reliability, which had been built up over more than forty years by a succession of talented and dedicated designers and engineers.

Left: 1997—the Corvette enters its seventh age. The turmoil that surrounded its gestation period is well documented in James Schefter's *All Corvettes are Red*, published in 1997.

Right: Radically restyled, yet instantly recognizable. The Seventh Generation Corvette represents a superb melding of tradition and innovation.

The stiff new chassis permitted an unprecedented standard of finish for the lithe new body shape. Panel fit was the best ever—always a bugbear with bolt-on panels, especially in GRP. The extensive employment of solid-state electronics benefited the car not only in terms of reliability, but by the fact that a vast amount of space, previously filled with cables and connectors, resistors and regulators was now freed up, providing yet more space for the driver and passenger. The same determination to rationalize and refine was applied to the panel work, resulting in fewer parts that simply fitted together better. Equipment levels were extremely high; the Corvette had come a long way from its Spartan youth. The dash panel display now included a tire-pressure monitor and warning as standard.

New openings

1998 saw the arrival of a new convertible. This was a completely new design but carried styling clues from earlier series that made it an instant hit, and orders accounted for a third of total output. The soft top incorporated a glass, heated rear window and negated the need for rear fixing by employing a lever/spring tensioning system that held the rear of the hood frame tight to the deck. The roof remained, as it always had been, manually operated. Once again, a certain level of pragmatism was evident in the Corvette's design. Many would view the lack of a power hood to be an outrageous omission on a near-fifty thousand dollar automobile. A true Corvetteer, on the other hand, would consider the consequences of hydraulic failure during a sudden cloudburst to be more important—when else would a hydraulic failure occur?

For the fourth time, the Corvette was chosen to be the pace car for the Indianapolis 500. The color scheme for the '98 was the wildest yet: purple with yellow wheels, a black hood and a black and yellow leather interior. Over 1,100 were produced, at $49,464 each—making this the most expensive Corvette convertible to date.

One of the most welcome innovations of the new convertible was the provision of a trunk lid! This convenience had not been seen on a ragtop 'Vette since the early sixties and was greeted with great enthusiasm. It even featured remote opening via a control button on the key fob.

A brand new handling package was offered, building on the improvements introduced in earlier series: Bosch anti-lock braking, in 1986, and ASR Traction Control in 1992. Now the JL4 Active Handling option was available for a mere $500. This system sensed any deviation from the intended cornering line by assessing and comparing the car's speed and direction

Below: The only thing that the seventh generation's LS1 engine had in common with its predecessor, the LT1, was its 350 cu.ins. displacement.

against the steering angle—all this in milliseconds. By applying anti-lock braking to any one of the wheels, either under- or over-steer could be corrected, almost imperceptibly. The system could be disabled for competition use, but for everyday driving represented yet another significant safety feature.

Right: The 1998 Corvette offered a full "Active Handling" adjustable suspension package for a mere $500.

Next Page: 1998 saw the appearance of a new convertible, complete with separate trunk— for the first time since 1962!

Right: For 1999, drivers could opt for a head-up display. Once again, aircraft technology was influencing the development of the Corvette.

Next Page: Over the years, the Corvette has won many admirers outside the USA. Details like individual tail light lenses allow for variations according to local custom.

1999

A hardtop 'Vette was added to the line in ninety-nine. The idea of making this an "entry-level" model, with bargain-basement fixtures and fittings, was, happily abandoned, but it was still the cheapest route to Corvette ownership, by just under four hundred dollars. The hardtop was not removable, but bonded to the bodywork, making the car even more rigid and purposeful in feel. To underline this, six-speed, manual transmission was provided as standard, along with the up-rated Z51 suspension. Interior options and paint colors were limited, further emphasizing the Hardtop's uncompromising character.

The styling of the earliest Corvettes was strongly influenced by Harley Earl's passion for aircraft design. He would have been greatly thrilled to see the introduction of a Head-Up Display option in 1999. This employed a specially developed windshield that produced an image of the main instruments, including the digital speed indicator, directly in the driver's eye-line. The brightness and position of the display were adjustable, as was the selection of information shown. The closest experience that drivers might have had prior to this, unless they'd served as fighter pilots, would have been during the reign of the sixties muscle cars, when a hood-mounted tacho could be specified on the Pontiac GTO...

Another feature from earlier days—Twilight Sentinel—had been featured on Cadillacs since the early seventies. This used a photo-electric sensor to determine when the ambient light had fallen to a level that required the showing of lights, and turned the lights on accordingly. One would have thought that a Corvette owner would have been sufficiently aware of his surroundings to at least register that it was getting dark, but then again it might be handy when driving through long, Alpine tunnels. Twilight Sentinel was a development of a system that dated from the fifties, which automatically dipped the lights when it sensed those of an on-coming vehicle and rejoiced in the name of the autronic-eye.

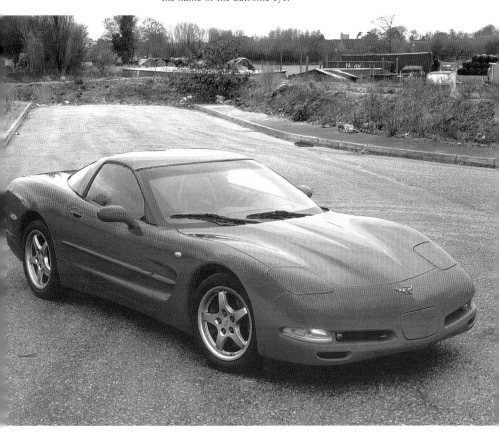

The New Millennium

Although each of the three
years leading up to the Big
2000 had seen the introduction
of a new model: the C5 coupe
in '97, the convertible in '98,
and the hardtop in '99, the
only innovation offered to greet
the dawn of the twenty-first
century was a unique color
finish: Millennium Yellow. This
$500 option featured a colored
lacquer layer over the base
coat, which gave the finish an
amazing depth and luster.
Millennium Yellow recalled the
color of the competition C5Rs
that had acquitted themselves
admirably in endurance races,
notable at Daytona, Sebring
and Le Mans.

Passive Keyless Entry
(PKE), which had been
introduced in 1993,
automatically unlocked or
locked the doors when it sensed
the approach or retreat of the
key fob. It had caused a certain
amount of irritation during
such operations as washing the
car, as it would sound the horn
to indicate that doors had

locked every time the owner retreated to the wash bucket or the hose tap. Never offered on export models, as its radio frequency might transgress local regulations, it was now deleted from the domestic options list. The wheels were restyled, with slimmer spokes, and the optional, magnesium Italian Speedlines were reduced in price from a jaw-slackening $3,000 to a merely outrageous $2,000.

Previous Page Main:
The wheel spokes of
the 2000 'Vette were
slimmed own to
produce a lighter,
more elegant look.

**Previous Page Top
Right:** Keyless entry
was abandoned in
2000, along with the
passenger side key
barrel.

**Previous Page
Bottom Right:** The
LS1 successor to the
trusty, iron small
block was 44 pounds
lighter and 45bhp
more powerful.

Right and Next Page:
From any angle, the
Millennium Corvette
is an object lesson in
integrated design. The
syling is purposeful
and yet restrained,
even in yellow.

Right: 2001 Corvettes shared the revised engine block design of the mighty LS6, raising output to 350bhp.

Z06

The Millennium celebrations were over and so another reason to get excited was provided in the shape of the Z06 option. This was a yet more *sportif* development of the hardtop and was fitted with a version of the LS1 tuned to 385bhp—more powerful than the '92 ZR1. This was given the designation LS6, recalling the mighty 425bhp, 427 cu.in., aluminum-headed big-block of 1971. The exterior was graced with stainless steel highlights, fully-operational rear brake vents and unique wheels that were even wider than those fitted to the coupe and the convertible, and were shod with Goodyear Eagle Supercar tires. These didn't run flat, like the EMT, and so a puncture repair kit was included in lieu of a spare. This was based on injecting a special, viscous solution into the tire and then inflating it with a canister of compressed air. The fluid automatically hardened and would plug the hole—at least long enough to get the car to a tire shop. As with the hardtop, exterior colors were limited—to black or black and red. The reworked engine block of the LS6 was fitted to the coupe and convertible also, raising their output by 5bhp to 350 without the need for any additional tuning. Now that the hardtop had been reinvented as the Z06, it was more expensive than the coupe. The red line was put 500rpm higher in the Z06, at 6500rpm. Production of both the LS1 and the LS6 was relocated to a facility in St. Catharines, Ontario, Canada.

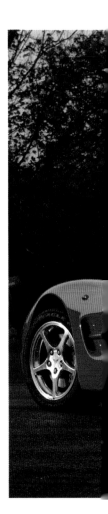

The Corvette paced the Indy 500 for the fifth time in 2002. This was appropriate as fourteen out of the fifteen cars that completed the course were powered by Chevrolet engines—including the first three finishers. Unlike previous Indy Pace Car years, no replicas were offered to the public. Three cars were built, as prototypes for the fiftieth anniversary model of 2003. For the statistically inclined, 2003 would be the fiftieth anniversary rather than the fifty-first as no cars were officially produced for one year between 1953 and 2003, that year being 1983.

The 2002 Z06 was rated at 405bhp. This was achieved by the removal of two of the pre-catalytic converters from the exhaust system. The induction was improved and hi-lift camshafts were installed, acting on lightweight valve-gear. Both intake and exhaust valves were formed hollow, and were filled with potassium and sodium alloy to aid heat dispersal.

Left: In 2002, the Corvette paced the Indy 500 for the fifth time. Three Pace Car Replicas was produced, anticipating the 50th anniversary model. Sadly, they were not for sale.

Right: By 2002, output of the standard Corvette was 350bhp, and the LS6 was good for over 400.

50 Up

The special Fiftieth Anniversary Corvette of 2003 is available as either a coupe or a convertible, finished in Anniversary Red with gold wheels and a two-tone Shale leather interior. All 2003 models feature the latest F55 Selective Magnetic Ride Control, which can calculate the vertical movement of each wheel one thousand times per second. The GM Delphi system uses a magnetic field, to control the viscosity of a synthetic fluid containing iron particles within the suspension dampers. By this method, the ride is monitored and adjusted twice for every inch of road covered at a speed of 60mph. How good can it get?

The 2003 Corvette shares its fiber glass body with its 1953 ancestor. It also shares the passion of the pioneers who designed and built it and the affection of the drivers who have owned and enjoyed it for half a century. The Corvette is perhaps the longest lived sports car in the world but it is, and will remain, forever young.

After half a century, the Corvette remains America's Number One performance automobile. It has fulfilled all the ambitions of '53 by becoming one of the finest sports cars in the world.

Next Page:
Despite its awesome complexity, the 2003 Corvette shares its GRP body panels and front-engine/rear-drive layout with the '53 model. Some things are simply unimprovable.

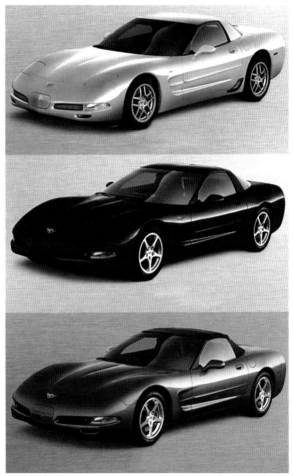

What makes the Corvette a great car is what makes America a great country: power with control.

CORVETTE TIME LINE 1953–2003

1953

June 30. The first Corvette comes off the line at Flint, Michigan. Like all the first batch, it is a Polo White Roadster with Sportsman Red interior. Transmission is via two-speed *Powerglide*. 0–60 = 11.0 sec. Top Speed = 106 mph.

Dwight D. Eisenhower is sworn in as 34th President of the United States

Elizabeth II is crowned Queen of England.

Hugh Heffner publishes *Playboy* magazine.

Ray Bradbury publishes *Fahrenheit 451*.

L. Ron Hubbard founds the Church of Scientology.

IBM introduces its first computer, the 701, with a capacity of 4kb.

Edmund Hilary and Sherpa Norkey Tenzing reach the summit of Everest.

Crick and Watson discover the double helix structure of DNA.

Ben Hogan wins the U.S. Open, the U.S. Masters and the British Open, becoming the first golfer to win three majors in one year.

The New York Yankees beat the Brooklyn Dodgers and become the first team to win the World Series five times in a row.

Josef Stalin dies.

Hank Williams dies.

Kim Basinger is born.

Tony Blair is born.

1954

Corvette production is switched to St. Louis, Missouri, where output reaches 600 cars a month, outstripping demand. The Corvette is now available in Pennant Blue and Sportsman Red as well as Polo White.

The fifty-millionth automobile to be built by an American manufacturer comes off the line, at Flint, Michigan – it's a Chevrolet.

The Mercedes-Benz 300 SL is the first car to feature fuel injection.

A study reveals that 80% of atmospheric pollution in the Greater Los Angeles area of California is caused by automobiles.

The U.S. National Cancer Institute links tobacco smoking to lung cancer.

America's first atomic power plant is built in Pittsburgh, Pennsylvania.

French troops surrender at Dien Bien Phu.

Marlon Brando stars in *The Wild One*.

J.R.R. Tolkien publishes *The Fellowship of the Ring*.

Marilyn Monroe marries Joe DiMaggio.

Marilyn Monroe sues for divorce.

Henri Matisse dies.

John Travolta is born.

1955

The Corvette is supplied with a 265cid, overhead-valve V8, producing 195bhp. New colors include Harvest Gold and Metallic Copper. 0–60 = 8.5 sec. Top Speed = 115mph. Only 674 cars are sold.

Marian Anderson becomes the first black singer to perform at the Metropolitan Opera House, New York.

Bill Haley and the Comets release *Rock Around the Clock*.

Chuck Berry releases *Maybelline*.

James Dean stars in *Rebel Without a Cause*.

J.R.R.Tolkien publishes *The Two Towers*.

Disneyland, the first theme park in the world, opens in Anaheim, California.

Lassie appears on U.S. television for the first time, along with *Champion, the Wonder Horse* and *The Phil Silvers Show*.

The United States Auto Club replaces the American Automobile Association as the governing body for Indy-car racing.

Louison Bobet of France becomes the first man to win the Tour de France three years in succession.

Willie Shoemaker wins his fifth Kentucky Derby, on Swaps.

Albert Einstein dies.

Charlie "Bird" Parker dies.

Kevin Costner is born.

Bill Gates in born.

1956

The Corvette is dramatically restyled and fitted with a close-ratio, three-speed, manual gearbox. The V8's output is increased to 225bhp. 0–60 = 7.5 sec. Top Speed = 120mph. Sales leap to 3,467.

Dwight D. Eisenhower is re-elected President of the United States.

Fidel Castro lands in Cuba

Felix Wankel invents the rotary engine.

The U.S. Congress passes the Federal Aid Highway Act, to permit the construction of 42,500 miles of interstate highway, to be funded by a tax on gasoline.

The General Motors Technical Centre opens, in Warren, Michigan.

Maria Callas debuts at the Metropolitan Opera House, New York.

Marilyn Monroe marries Arthur Miller.

Grace Kelly marries Prince Rainier of Monaco.

Yul Brynner stars in *The King and I*.

J.R.R.Tolkien publishes *The Return of the King*.

Elvis Presley releases *Hound Dog*.

Doris Day releases *Que sera, sera*.

William E. Boeing dies.

Tom Hanks is born.

1957

The Corvette gets "Ramjet" fuel-injection and four-speed, manual transmission. Bored out to 283cid, the V8's power output is increased to a maximum of 283bhp. 0–60 = 5.7 sec. Top Speed = 132mph.

President Dwight D. Eisenhower is inaugurated for a second term and the public ceremonies are videotaped and become the first nationally-broadcast item.

The U.S.S.R. launches *Sputnik 1*, the world's first artificial satellite.

Evangelist Billy Graham concludes a four-month tour of the United States.

Juan Manuel Fangio becomes the first man to be Formula One World Champion four times in a row.

Althea Gibson of the United States becomes the first black player to win a singles title at the Wimbledon Lawn Tennis championships in England.

Sony produce the first miniature transistor radio.

Smith-Corona produce the first portable electric typewriter.

Henry Fonda stars in *Twelve Angry Men*.

Grant Williams stars in *The Incredible Shrinking Man*.

Ian Fleming publishes *From Russia With Love*.

Boris Pasternak publishes *Doktor Zhivago*.

The Everly Brothers release *Bye Bye Love*.

Senator Joe McCarthy and Eliot Ness die.

Humphrey Bogart dies.

Seve Ballesteros and Nick Faldo are born.

1958

Corvette fuel-injected horsepower reaches 290 and so exceeds 1hp per cubic inch. Sales and chromium increase proportionally. Entry-level price is kept low at $3631, but the model shows a profit for the first time.

Bank Americard is launched, the first true credit card.

Chairman Mao instigates China's *Great Leap Forward*.

The National Aeronautics and Space Administration (NASA) is created.

National Airlines introduces the first non-stop service between New York and Miami.

Bell Laboratories produce the first modem, which permits a telephone line to carry information in binary form and is the first step to creating the World Wide Web.

American Jack Kilby demonstrates the first integrated circuit. It consists of a silicone substrate containing transistors, resistors and capacitors and leads to the third generation of computers.

Steve McQueen stars in *The Blob*.

Maurice Chevalier and Leslie Caron star in *Gigi*.

Perry Como releases *Magic Moments*.

Elvis Presley begins two years military service.

Pope Pius XII dies.

Tyrone Power dies.

Michelle Pfieffer is born.

Michael Jackson is born.

1959

Harley Earl, father of the Corvette, retires as head of styling at General Motors. Chromium trim is deleted and rear suspension is revised to cope with ever-increasing power output.

Alaska becomes the 49th State of the Union and Hawaii becomes the 50th State of the Union.

Oklahoma repeals prohibition.

Soviet leader Nikita Krushchev visits the United States.

The U.S. Navy launches *Vanguard 2*, the world's first weather satellite.

The Guggenheim Museum, designed by Frank Lloyd Wright, opens in New York.

Ed Wood Jnr's *Plan 9 from Outer Space* is released.

Ian Fleming publishes *Goldfinger*.

Bobby Darin releases *Mack the Knife*.

The Barbie Doll goes on sale.

Rawhide appears on U.S. TV for the first time, featuring Clint Eastwood.

The Untouchables appears on U.S. TV for the first time, starring Robert Stack.

Ingemar Johansson knocks out Floyd Patterson to become heavyweight champion of the world.

Lee Petty, driving an Oldsmobile 88, wins the inaugural Daytona 500.

C. B. De Mille, Buddy Holly, Raymond Chandler, Errol Flynn, General George C. Marshall and Frank Lloyd Wright die.

John McEnroe is born.

1960

Corvette production exceeds 10,000 for the first time. Compression on top fuel-injected models rises to 11:1. Max. output is now 315bhp. Options include a 24 gallon fuel tank and competition suspension. The Corvette dominates sports car racing as Briggs Cunningham's team place 8th at Le Mans.

Chrysler discontinues the De Soto line after 42 years of production.

The Organisation of Petroleum Exporting Countries (OPEC) meets for the first time, in Iraq, and raises the price of oil.

The United States imposes an export embargo on Cuba.

John F. Kennedy is elected president by the narrowest margin in history with 49.7% against 49.6% for Richard M. Nixon.

The State of California approves the U.S.'s first anti-smog legislation.

Paul Newman and Eve Marie Saint star in *Exodus*.

Anthony Perkins, Vera Miles and Janet Leigh star in *Psycho*.

The Beatles release *She Loves You*.

Elvis Presley releases *Are You Lonesome Tonight?*

Harper Lee publishes *To Kill a Mockingbird*.

The U.S. flag gets 50 stars.

Floyd Patterson regains the world heavyweight boxing championship by defeating Ingemar Johansson.

Cassius Clay wins the light-heavyweight boxing gold medal at the Olympic Games in Rome.

John D. Rockefeller dies.

Ayrton Senna is born.

1961

The Corvette's tail and radiator grille are restyled. Fuel-injected cars can run 0–60mph in 5.5 seconds and have a top speed in excess of 130mph.

Adolf Eichmann is tried in Israel for war crimes, convicted and sentenced to death.

John F. Kennedy is sworn in as 35th – and youngest ever – U.S. President.

The *Bay of Pigs* invasion, by U.S.-trained, Cuban exiles, fails.

The first American troops land in Vietnam.

IBM introduces the electronic "Golf Ball" typewriter.

Mattel Toys launch Ken, a boyfriend for Barbie.

Alan Sheppard becomes the first U.S. astronaut in space.

Edward Lorenz comes up with the Chaos Theory

Charlton Heston and Sophia Loren star in *El Cid*.

Clark Gable, Marilyn Monroe and Montgomery Clift star in *The Misfits*.

Yevgeny Yevtushenko publishes his poem *Babi Yar*.

Joseph Heller publishes his novel *Catch-22*.

Bobby Vee releases *Poetry in Motion*.

The Dick Van Dyke Show appears on U.S. TV for the first time.

Dr. Kildare appears on U.S. TV for the first time, starring Richard Chamberlain.

Ernest Hemingway commits suicide.

Lady Diana Spencer (later Princess Diana) is born.

1962

Corvette 283cid engines are bored out to 327cid. Maximum power output rises to 360bhp. Two-tone accenting on the side coves is deleted. Dick Thompson, *The Flying Dentist*, wins the SCCA A-Production title in a Corvette. Production increases to 14,500.

The U.S. National Debt passes the $300 billion mark.

U2 Pilot Gary Powers is released by the Russians in exchange for Soviet spy Rudolf Abel.

Nelson Mandela is sentenced to five years imprisonment in South Africa for inciting workers to strike.

The Cuban Missile Crisis brings the U.S. and U.S.S.R. close to war.

Telstar, the first U.S. telecommunications satellite, is launched.

Dr. No, the first James Bond movie, directed by Terence Young, is released.

How the West Was Won, directed by John Ford, is released.

Anthony Burgess's *A Clockwork Orange* is published.

Ken Kesey's *One Flew Over the Cuckoo's Nest* is published.

Bob Dylan releases *Blowin' in the Wind*.

The Beach Boys release *Surfin' Safari*.

Philip Morris introduces the Marlboro Cowboy.

The Beverley Hillbillies appear on U.S. TV for the first time.

Sonny Liston defeats Floyd Patterson to become heavyweight boxing champion of the world.

Marilyn Monroe dies.

Jodie Foster is born.

1963

Bill Mitchell's Corvette *Sting Ray* is introduced, with a new, ladder-frame chassis designed by Zora Arkus-Duntov. The radically restyled new model is shorter, narrower and lighter than its predecessor, The divided rear window of the new coupe proves controversial. Sales double.

Martin Luther King Jr. addresses around two hundred thousand people in Washington DC, delivering the famous "*I have a dream...*" speech.

President John F. Kennedy addresses around two hundred thousand people in West Berlin, delivering the famous "*Ich bin ein Berliner*" speech.

Frank Sinatra Jr. is kidnapped in Lake Tahoe, Nevada, and ransomed for a quarter of a million dollars, which is paid by his father.

The United States now has 6% of the world's population and 66% of the world's automobiles.

Kodak introduces the first *Instamatic* camera.

Sean Connery stars as James Bond in *From Russia With Love.*

Elizabeth Taylor stars as Cleopatra in *Cleopatra.*

The Beatles release *Please Please Me.*

Frank Sinatra releases *Fly Me to the Moon.*

The Fugitive, starring David Janssen, appears on U.S. TV for the first time.

Arnold Palmer becomes the first golfer to win over a million dollars in a season.

The Chicago Bears win a record seventh NFL title.

President John F. Kennedy is assassinated in Dallas, Texas.

1964

The Corvette Sting Ray loses its fake hood louvers. Top power for the fuelie rises to 375bhp. Coupe rear window divide is deleted. Options now include leather upholstery, power steering, power brakes, air-conditioning and stereo.

Lyndon B. Johnson is now the 36th President of the United States.

U.S. warships are attacked off the coast of North Vietnam.

Martin Luther King Jnr. wins the Nobel Prize for Peace.

The Varrazano Narrows Suspension Bridge, between Staten Island and Brooklyn, is opened. It has the longest single span in the world, at 4,258ft.

Stanley Kubrick's *Dr. Strangelove*, or How I learned to *Stop Worrying and Love the Bomb*, is released.

George Cukor's *My Fair Lady* is released.

Richard Burton and Elizabeth Taylor marry in Montreal, Canada.

Both the Chrysler Corporation and the Ford Motor Corporation succeed in agreeing deals with the UAW, but General Motors fails and production is severely disrupted by strikes.

The Addams Family appear on U.S. TV for the first time.

The Man from U.N.C.L.E. appears on Us TV for the first time.

Cassius Clay defeats Sonny Liston to become the heavyweight boxing champion of the world. Clay then converts to Islam and changes his name to Muhammad Ali.

Englishman Donald Campbell becomes the first man to hold both the world's land speed record and the water speed record.

General Douglas MacArthur, Herbert Hoover and Cole Porter die.

Keanu Reeves is born.

1965

Roger Penske takes a class win in a Corvette at Nassau. The big-block V8 is introduced, initially at 396cid, later 427cid. Clutch, cooling and suspension are all up-rated to deal with the 425bhp output.

Malcolm X is shot dead in New York

Race riots erupt in the Watts district of Los Angeles, California.

U.S. soldiers enter the war in Vietnam for the first time at Danang.

U.S. aircraft bomb North Vietnam in *Operation Rolling Thunder*.

Congress orders that all cigarette packets sold in the U.S. must carry a health warning.

The Highway Beautification Act bans roadside advertising.

Ralph Nader publishes *Unsafe at any Speed*.

David Lean's *Doctor Zhivago* is released.

Robert Wise's *The Sound of Music* is released.

Bob Dylan plays electric guitar at the Newport Folk Festival.

Pope Paul VI celebrates mass at Yankee Stadium.

Timothy Leary coins the phrase "Turn on, tune in, drop out."

Allan Ginsberg coins the expression "Flower power."

Riding an MV Agusta, English motorcyclist Mike Hailwood wins his fourth successive 500cc world championship.

Driving a Lotus, Scottish racing driver Jim Clark is the first European to win the Indianapolis 500 since Louis Chevrolet, in 1920.

Winston Churchill, Albert Schweitzer and Adlai Stevenson die.

Bjork is born.

1966

A 427cid, Corvette Mark IV can hit 60mph in under five seconds and has a top speed of over 140mph. Sales approach 28,000.

LSD is declared illegal in the United States.

U.S. troops in Vietnam number over four hundred thousand.

The minimum wage is increased from $1.25 to $1.40 per hour.

The U.S. coastal fishing limit is increased from three to twelve miles.

Clint Eastwood and Lee Van Cleef star in *The Good, the Bad and the Ugly*.

Lee Marvis wins an Academy Award as Best Actor Oscar for *Cat Ballou*.

Frank Sinatra sings *Strangers in the Night*.

Nancy Sinatra sings *These Boots are Made for Walkin'*.

John Lennon opines that the Beatles are more popular than Jesus.

The Monkees are created.

Batman appears on U.S. TV for the first time.

Tarzan appears on U.S. TV for the first time.

England beat West Germany to win the soccer world cup at Wembley, England.

Muhammad Ali beats Cleveland Williams to retain the world heavyweight boxing championship.

Walt Disney dies.

Janet Jackson is born.

1967

Introduction of the new Corvette is delayed due to development problems, allowing the Sting Ray to enjoy an "Indian Summer." Embellishment is reduced to zero. The Corvette never looked better.

Expo '76 opens in Montreal, Canada.

The Six Day War begins and ends in victory for Israel.

Virgil Grissom , Edward White II and Roger Chaffee become the first fatalities of the U.S. space program in Apollo 1.

Vladimir Komarov becomes the first fatality of the U.S.S.R. space program, in Soyuz 1.

Dr. Christiaan Barnard performs the first heart transplant operation, in South Africa.

Dr. Adrian Kantrowitz performs the first heart transplant operation in the U.S.

The first, domestic microwave oven goes on sale in the U.S.

Mazda of Japan produce the first rotary-engined car.

The liner Queen Elizabeth II is launched on the River Clyde, Scotland.

Warren Beatty and Faye Dunaway star in *Bonnie and Clyde*.

Dustin Hoffman and Anne Bancroft star in *The Graduate*.

John Boorman directs *Point Blank*.

The Beatles release *Sgt. Peppers Lonely Hearts Club Band*.

The Jimi Hendrix Experience release *Are You Experienced*?

Che Guevara dies.

Kurt Cobain is born.

1968

The Fifth Generation Corvette is announced and is branded "unfit to test" by one reviewer. Its striking appearance is marred by poor quality control. Despite the criticisms, sales reach an all time high of 28,500.

The United Auto Workers Union mergers with the Teamsters to form the Alliance for Labor Action

Feminists demonstrate against the Miss America pageant in Atlantic City, New Jersey.

Lyndon B. Johnson orders the cessation of the bombing of North Vietnam.

Stanley Kubrik's *2001: A Space Odyssey* is released.

Peter Yate's *Bullitt* is released.

The 911 emergency telephone service is introduced.

The Jacuzzi Brothers introduce their first "whirlpool bath."

Rowan and Martin's Laugh-In appears on U.S. television.

U.S. athletes Tommie Smith and John Carlos give "Black Power" salutes from the winners rostrum of the Olympic Games in Mexico City

Muhammad Ali is stripped of his world heavyweight boxing title for refusing to be drafted into the army.

Martin Luther King is assassinated in Memphis, Tennessee.

Robert Kennedy is assassinated in Los Angeles, California.

Yuri Gagarin, the first man in space, dies in an jet plane crash near Moscow.

Jim Clark, world champion racing driver, dies in a race car crash at Hockenheim.

1969

The Stingray name is reintroduced, as one word. Much work is done to correct design flaws and increase cockpit space. Emission control prompts the lowering of compression ratios. The quarter-of-a-millionth Corvette is produced at St. Louis, Missouri.

Richard M. Nixon is sworn in as 37th president of the U.S.

Senator Edward Kennedy drives off a bridge at Cappaquiddick Island. His passenger, Mary Jo Kopechne, drowns.

Apollo 11 lands on the moon. Neil Armstrong makes "… one small step for a man, one giant leap for mankind."

Charles Manson and his followers murder actress Sharon Tate and others at the home of her husband, film director Roman Polanski, in Bel Air, California.

Dennis Hopper's *Easy Rider* is released.

George Roy Hill's *Butch Cassidy and the Sundance Kid* is released.

Mario Puzo publishes *The Godfather*.

Kurt Vonnegut publishes *Slaughterhouse Five*.

Frank Sinatra releases *My Way*.

Leonard Cohen releases *Songs From A Room*.

500,000 people go to listen to the music at Woodstock.

Hell's Angels kill a fan at Altamont.

Penthouse goes on sale for the first time.

Sesame Street goes on TV for the first time.

Dwight Eisenhower, Ho Chi Minh and Judy Garland die.

Sean "P. Diddy" Combs is born.

1970

Corvette production drops by half due to a prolonged auto-workers strike. To compensate for the drop in compression ratios, the big block engine gets even bigger, up to 454 cu.ins. The solid-lifter, 370 bhp, LT1 version of the small block is introduced. Design details continue to be revised and refined.

U.S. troop withdrawals from Vietnam continue. 150,000 U.S. service personnel come home.

The National Guard fires on student demonstrators at Kent State University, Ohio, killing four.

IBM introduces the "floppy disc" for computer data storage.

Canon Business Systems produce the first pocket calculator.

The U.S. military initiates the GPS (Global Positioning System) for navigation, utilizing 21 satellites.

The north tower of the World Trade Center in New York is completed. At 1,350ft., it is the tallest building on earth.

M.A.S.H. wins the Palme d'Or at the Cannes Film Festival.

John Wayne wins the Best Actor Oscar for *True Grit*.

Simon and Garfunkel release *Bridge Over Troubled Water*.

Richard Bach publishes *Jonathan Livingston Seagull*.

Cigarette advertising is banned on radio and TV in the U.S.

Joe Frazier becomes the undisputed heavyweight champion of the world.

Gary Gabelich takes the world land speed record in his *Blue Flame*, rocket powered car at Bonneville Salt Flats, Utah.

Jimi Hendrix dies.

River Phoenix is born.

1971

Corvette sales rise to 21,801, having fallen well below 20,000 in the previous year. Economic uncertainty, emission legislation, rising gasoline prices and insurance premiums all conspire against the manufacture and sale of high performance autos.

The 26th Amendment to the Constitution gives the vote to eighteen year olds.

The environmental protest group *Greenpeace* is founded.

An earthquake kills 51 people in Los Angeles, California.

Tornadoes kill over 100 people in Mississippi and Louisiana.

Floods kill more than 100,000 people in North Vietnam.

Quadraphonic stereo is introduced.

Rolls Royce Motors goes bankrupt.

Stanley Kubrick's *A Clockwork Orange* is released.

Peter Bogdanovitch's *The Last Picture Show* is released.

Stephen Spielberg's TV movie *Duel* is broadcast.

Disney World opens in Orlando, Florida.

Joe Frazier beats Muhammad Ali to retain his world heavyweight boxing title.

A U.S. table-tennis team plays a series of matches in the People's Republic of China.

Al Unser wins his second Indy 500 at an average speed of over 157mph.

The LA Lakers set a record of 27 consecutive NBA wins.

Louis Armstrong, Jim Morrison and Igor Stravinsky die.

Pete Sampras is born.

1972

Horsepower ratings are switched from gross to net (SAE) which made them seem even lower, thus the output of '72's most powerful engine appears to be equal to '71's least powerful, at 270bhp. The LS-6 engine option is deleted.

The U.S.S.R. begins bulk-purchase of surplus grain from the U.S.

Governor George Wallace is shot and paralyzed at a political meeting in Maryland.

Bob Woodward and Carl Bernstein of the *Washington Post* report s break-in at the Democratic Party HQ in the Watergate Hotel complex, Washington DC.

Polaroid introduce the SX-70 their first color camera system.

Federal Express is founded.

Marlon Brando stars in *The Godfather*.

Gene Hackman stars in *The Poseidon Adventure*.

Lisa Minelli stars in *Cabaret*.

The Waltons first appears on U.S. TV.

British racing driver Graham Hill becomes the first person to have won the Formula 1 World Championship, the Indianapolis 500 and the La Mans 24 hour race.

U.S. Golfer Jack Nicklaus wins his third U.S. Open Championship.

U.S. swimmer Mark Spitz wins seven gold medals at the Munich Olympic Games.

11 Israeli athletes are murdered by Arab terrorists at the Munich Olympic Games.

J. Edgar Hoover, Charles Atlas, King Edward VIII and Maurice Chevalier die.

1973

The Corvette gets an impact-resistant "soft nose" and improvements to the chassis mounts. Engine options are reduced to two 350s and one 454. Sales climb back above 30,000.

Richard Milhous Nixon is sworn in for a second term as president.

OPEC announce a doubling in the price of oil.

The last U.S. troops are evacuated from Vietnam.

U.S. Secretary of State Henry Kissinger and founder member of the Indochinese Communist Party, Le Duc Tho, share the Nobel Prize for peace.

Egypt and Syria attack Israel on the Jewish holy day of Yom Kippur.

The U.S. agrees to grant two billion dollars worth of military aid to Israel.

The Sears Tower is Chicago, Illinois, becomes the world's tallest building, at 1,454ft. The World Trade Center in New York is completed.

George Lucas's *American Graffiti* is released.

William Friedkin's *The Exorcist* is released.

Elton John releases *Goodbye, Yellow Brick Road*.

George Foreman defeats Joe Frazier to become world heavyweight boxing champion.

O. J. Simpson of the Buffalo Bills becomes the first football player to gain more than 2000 yards (2003) by rushing in a season.

Lyndon B. Johnson and Edward G. Robinson die.

1974

Zora Arkus-Duntov retires. The LT-1 and the big block engine options are deleted. The Corvette gets an impact-absorbing tail section to match its "soft" nose. Times are tough for sports cars but Corvette sales climb steadily.

President Richard M. Nixon resigns to avoid impeachment over the Watergate affair.

Gerald Rudolph Ford is sworn in as the 38th president of the United States.

Brazil introduces a new automobile fuel, known as *alcool*, a mixture of gasoline and ethyl alcohol distilled from sugar.

The Arab oil embargo against the United States is lifted.

The first laser-read barcodes appear in U.S. supermarkets.

Robert Redford stars in *The Great Gatsby*.

Jack Nicholson stars in *Chinatown*.

Robert M. Pirsig publishes *Zen and the Art of Motorcycle Maintenance*.

Happy Days appears on U.S. TV.

Hank Aaron of the Atlanta Braves beats Babe Ruth's record of 714 home runs that had stood since 1935.

Belgian cyclist Eddy Merckx becomes the first rider to win the Tour de France, the Giro d'Italia and the World Road Race Championship in the same season.

Muhammad Ali defeats George Foreman to regain the world heavyweight boxing title.

Little girls are permitted to play baseball in the Little League for the first time.

Errett Lobban Cord dies.

1975

Dave McLellan becomes Corvette chief engineer and vows to retain the traditional front-engine-rear-drive layout, although much time, effort and money has been spent on experimental, mid-engined prototypes. The Corvette remains virtually unchanged, as do sales, though they now approach 40,000.

GM is overtaken by Exxon (formerly Standard Oil) as America's richest company.

William Henry Gates III founds a company called Microsoft.

Staff are evacuated by helicopter from the roof of the U.S. Embassy in Saigon.

Two assassination attempts is made against president Ford.

The Suez canal reopens.

Liquid Crystal Displays (LCDs) appear.

Jimmy Hoffa disappears.

The first Drive-Thru McDonald's opens.

Over a quarter of a million U.S. auto workers are laid off.

Steven Spielberg's *Jaws* is released.

Jim Sharman's *The Rocky Horror Picture Show* is released.

Saturday Night Live appears on U.S. TV.

Billie Jean King wins the ladies singles tennis championship at Wimbledon.

Arthur Ashe wins the men's singles tennis championship at Wimbledon.

Aristotle Onassis, 2nd husband of Jackie Kennedy, dies.

Graham Hill dies.

1976

In Bicentennial Year there is no Corvette Roadster for the first time since the model was introduced in 1953 and, at the end of the year, the Stingray name was finally abandoned. Sales rise to over forty-six and a half thousand.

Vietnam is reunified.

Israeli special forces rescue over a hundred hijack hostages from Entebbe, Uganda.

U.S. *Viking* spacecraft land on Mars.

The Anglo-French *Concorde* supersonic airliner enters service.

A Lockheed "Blackbird" sets a jet speed record of over 2000 miles per hour.

Alex Haley publishes *Roots*.

The Eagles release *Hotel California*.

Sony introduces the Betamax video-cassette recorder.

JVC introduce the VHS video-cassette recorder.

Charlie's Angels appear on U.S. TV for the first time.

Laverne & Shirley appear on U.S. TV for the first time.

29 members of the American Legion die of an unknown illness contracted at a congress in Philadelphia. The infection is dubbed Legionnaire's Disease.

Austrian driver Nikki Lauda is severely injured in a crash at the German Grand Prix.

Sissy Spacek stars in *Carrie*.

Sylvester Stallone stars in *Rocky*.

John Paul Getty and Mao Tse Tung die.

1977

Bill Mitchell retires and the mid-engined *Aerovette* concept is quietly shelved. Rotary motors have been tried and found wanting; the 350 small block soldiers on and sales come close to 50,000.

Jimmy Carter is sworn in as the 39th president of the United States.

Apple launches the first personal computer.

New York experiences a twenty-four hour power cut.

California makes the fitting of catalytic exhaust converters to all new automobiles mandatory.

Laker Airways provides a New York – London round-trip service for $100.00

Close Encounters of the Third Kind is released.

Saturday Night Fever is released.

Star Wars is released.

Fleetwood Mac release *Rumours*.

Meat Loaf release *Bat Out of Hell*.

Alex Haley's *Roots* is screened over eight nights on U.S. TV.

The Love Boat appears on U.S. TV for the first time.

A. J. Foyt becomes the first driver to win the Indy 500 four times.

Jockey Steve Cauthen makes over six million dollars prize money in his first season.

Charlie Chaplin dies.

Elvis Presley, Bing Crosby and Maria Callas die.

1978

The Corvette, celebrating its 25th birthday, gets a completely new, wrap-around, rear window treatment. A commemorative Silver Anniversary Edition is produced, plus an Indy Pace Car Replica.

Ben Cohen and Jerry Greenfield open an ice cream parlour in Vermont.

The dollar rises sharply after U.S. president Jimmy Carter announces a major support plan, including higher interest rates.

Cleveland, Ohio, defaults on its debts, the first U.S. city to do so since the 1930s depression.

The Ford Motor Corporation is fined over a hundred million in lawsuits over a flawed filler-neck and fuel tank design.

CFCs, gases used as propellants in aerosols, are banned in the U.S.

Apple Computers unveil personal computers with disc drives.

The first "test tube" baby is born in London, England.

John Irving publishes *The World According to Garp*.

Robert De Niro stars in *The Deer Hunter*.

Christopher Reeve stars in *Superman*.

Village People release *YMCA* and *In the Navy*.

Evita opens in London.

Taxi appears on U.S. TV.

Mork and Mindy appear on U.S. TV.

Dallas appears on U.S. TV.

Norman Rockwell dies.

1979

Corvette equipment now includes stereo, adjustable steering column, power windows and door locks in the base price. The Corvette's base price is now $12,313. Sales exceed 50,000.

The price of oil doubles due to revolution in Iran.

The Chrysler Corporation requires financial assistance from the federal government to save it from bankruptcy.

Margaret Thatcher becomes Britain's first woman prime minister.

Ayatollah Khomeini becomes leader in Iran.

The U.S. embassy in Tripoli, Libya, is burned.

Soviet troops invade Afghanistan.

The Rubik Cube goes on sale in the U.S.

The Post-it sticker goes on sale in the U.S.

The Sony Walkman goes on sale in the U.S.

Ridley Scott's *Alien* is released.

Francis Ford Coppola's *Apocalypse Now* is released.

Peter Sellers stars in *Being There*.

Mel Gibson stars in *Mad Max*.

The Dukes of Hazzard appears on U.S. TV.

Hart to Hart appears on U.S. TV.

Rick Mears wins the first Champion Auto Racing Teams (CART) World Series.

Fuzzy Zoeller wins the Master golf tournament at his first attempt.

Sid Vicious and Mary Pickford die.

1980

The Corvette sheds 150lbs., largely through the use of aluminum parts in place of steel. The spoilers from the Indy Pace Car Replica are incorporated into the nose and tail to improve aerodynamics. Production drops by over 13,000.

The General Motors Corporation declares a loss for the first time since 1921.

The Iran–Iran war breaks out.

IBM develops a voice-recognition system that can display words on the computer screen at the speed at which they are spoken.

Carl Sagan publishes *Cosmos*.

Tom Wolfe publishes *The Right Stuff*.

Stanley Kubrick's *The Shining* is released

Martin Scorsese's *Raging Bull* is released.

John Landis's *The Blues Brothers* is released.

Irvin Kershner's *The Empire Strikes Back* is released.

Cable News Network (CNN) goes on air, 24 hours a day.

Dallas breaks all existing ratings when the "Who Killed J.R.?" episode is broadcast on television, and watched by over 114 million people.

Twenty-three year-old Severiano Ballesteros becomes the youngest ever winner of the U.S. Masters golf tournament.

Johnny Rutherford wins his third Indy 500.

Mae West and Peters Sellers die.

John Lennon is murdered in New York.

1981

Corvette sales steady at around 40,600. Weight-saving measures continue with the literal "slimming down" of GRP body panels and window glass. A fiberglass rear leaf spring is adopted. A new version of the 350 cu.ins. small block is introduced: the L-81 uses a computer-controlled engine management system.

Ronald Reagan is sworn in as 40th president of the United States.

Iran releases 52 U.S. hostages they have held for over a year.

President Reagan is wounded in an assassination attempt

Pope John Paul II is wounded in an assassination attempt.

IBM launch their first PC using the Microsoft MS-DOS operating system.

The FDA approves Nutrasweet.

The U.S. government lends the Chrysler Corporation $400 million.

Striking U.S. air-traffic controllers are fired when they refuse to return to work.

MTV goes on air for the first time.

John Boorman's *Excalibur* is released.

Steven Spielberg's *Raiders of the Lost Ark* is released.

Charles, Prince of Wales, marries Lady Diana Spencer.

Dynasty appears on U.S. TV.

Driver Richard Petty wins the Daytona 500 for the seventh time.

Jockey Bill Shoemaker rides his eight thousandth winner.

Joe Louis and Bob Marley die.

1982

Corvette production has now been relocated to an exclusive, purpose built facility at Bowling Green, Kentucky. A new model from the new factory is keenly anticipated. Sales slip to a ten-year low of 25,407. Japanese cars now account for nearly a quarter of the U.S. market.

The DeLorean car factory in Northern Ireland closes.

Apple Computers achieve sales of a billion dollars.

Argentina invades the British colony of the Falkland Islands, British troops expel the invaders. Losses total: 255 British; 652 Argentine.

The Vietnam War Memorial in Washington is unveiled. It lists the names of over 58,000 U.S. service personnel, killed or missing.

Kodak produces the first digital camera.

Sony produce the first CD player.

Graceland opens to the public in Memphis, Tennessee.

EPCOT opens to the public in Lake Buena Vista, Florida.

Arnold Schwarzenegger stars in *Conan the Barbarian*.

Dustin Hoffman stars in *Tootsie*.

Michael Jackson's *Thriller* is the best selling album of all time.

Madonna appears on MTV for the first time.

USA Today appears on U.S. news stands for the first time.

Cheers appears on U.S. TV for the first time.

The first bicycle Race Across America is won by Lon Haldeman, covering nearly 3,000 miles in just under ten days.

John Belushi and Grace Kelly die.

1984

A Sixth Generation Corvette, built on a "backbone" chassis, with completely new running gear, is released. Powered by the L-83 incarnation of the 350 small block, with "Cross-Fire" fuel injection, it is more aerodynamically efficient and roomier than its predecessor.

Over 70 American banks collapse.

Arab terrorists attack the U.S. embassy in Beirut.

Irish terrorists attack the Grand Hotel in Brighton, England, where the prime minister, Margaret Thatcher, is staying.

Apple launch the *Macintosh* personal computer.

The CD-ROM is introduced.

Union Carbide pay nearly half a billion dollars in damages when a chemical leak at their factory in Bhopal, India, kills more than 2,500 people.

San Francisco bath houses are closed in an attempt to halt the spread of the AIDS virus amongst the gay community.

Miami Vice appears on U.S. TV.

Bruce Springsteen releases *Born in the USA*.

Madonna releases *Like a Virgin*.

Harrison Ford stars in *Indiana Jones and the Temple of Doom*.

Arnold Schwarzenegger stars in *The Terminator*.

Rick Mears wins the Indy 500

Laurent Fignon wins the Tour de France

Marvin Gaye dies.

Prince Harry is born.

1985

The complex, fuel-saving, "4+3" gearbox designed by Doug Nash proves controversial... Fuel injection is changed from "Cross-Fire" to "Tuned-Port" and 25bhp is gained. Suspension is revised for improved ride.

Soviet leader Mikhail Gorbachev announces the need for glasnost (transparency) in government policy.

President Reagan announces increases spending on the so-called *Star Wars* defense system to $26,000,000,000.

The IRS uses computers to process tax returns for the first time.

A hole in the Earth's ozone layer is detected above Antarctica.

The Greenpeace vessel *Rainbow Warrior* is blown up by French secret agents whilst anchored in New Zealand.

Palestinian hijackers seize the Italian cruise ship *Achille Lauro*.

The wreck of the Titanic is discovered.

A DeLorean appears in Robert Zemeckis's *Back to the Future*.

John Lennon's Rolls Royce is sold for three million dollars.

Live Aid concerts raise over seventy million dollars to feed the starving in Africa.

Pictures of missing children appear on U.S. milk cartons

The Golden Girls appear on U.S. TV.

Danny Sullivan wins the Indy 500

Bernard Hinault wins the Tour de France.

Clarence Nash, voice of Donald Duck for nearly 50 years, dies.

Orson Welles dies.

1986

The roadster returns. After a decade's absence, a fully convertible Corvette is offered once more. Bosch anti-lock brakes are fitted as standard equipment. The L-98 small block gets aluminum cylinder heads and a higher compression ratio.

General Motors is once more the richest company in the United States.

Wall Street suffers the worst fall in share prices since the crash of '29.

A Russian nuclear power plant at Chernobyl explodes.

A plant for irradiating fruit is opened in New Jersey.

Nintendo launches *Super Mario Brothers*.

Garrison Keillor publishes *Lake Wobegon Days*.

Tom Cruise stars in *Top Gun*.

Sigourney Weaver stars in *Aliens*.

Paul Simon releases *Graceland*.

Run DMC release *Raisin' Hell*.

Willie Shoemaker (54) becomes the oldest Jockey to win the Kentucky Derby

Ray Floyd (43) becomes the oldest golfer to win the U.S. Open.

Mike Tyson (20) becomes the youngest boxer to win the WBC heavyweight title.

Greg Lemond becomes the first American cyclist to win the Tour de France.

Oliver North is fired.

Otto Preminger dies.

1987

Roller valve lifters help to push the Corvette's power output to 240bhp. Sales hover around 30,000, of which about a third are convertibles. Base prices are now $27,999 for the coupe and $33,172 for the roadster.

On "Black Monday" (Oct. 19) the Dow Jones index falls by over five hundred points, almost a quarter of its value.

The U.S. dollar is at an all-time low on world currency markets.

An Iraqi missile strikes the *USS Stark*, on patrol in the Persian Gulf.

A German teenager lands a micro light aircraft in Moscow's Red Square.

The FDA approves AZT as a treatment for AIDS.

The FDA approves Prozac as a treatment for depression.

Margaret Thatcher is elected British prime minister for the third time.

Stanley Kubrick's *Full Metal Jacket* is released.

Barry Levinson's *Good Morning, Vietnam* is released.

Michael Douglas and Glenn Close star in *Fatal Attraction*.

Michael Douglas and Charlie Sheen star in *Wall Street*.

Tom Wolfe publishes *Bonfire of the Vanities*.

Irish cyclist Stephen Roche emulates Eddy Merckx by winning the Tour de France, the Giro d'Italia and the World Road Race Championship in the same year.

U.S. Basketball player Michael Jordan emulates Wilt Chamberlain by scoring 3000 points in a season.

Liberace and Andy Warhol die.

1988

Having missed out on a 30th birthday party, the Corvette celebrated its 35th with a limited edition anniversary model. Suspension was improved on all cars to reduce dive and squat, under braking and acceleration respectively.

The U.S. national debt exceeds a trillion dollars ($1,000,000,000,000).

Wall Street suffers the largest single-day loss in its history.

McDonalds open their ten thousandth outlet.

George Bush is nominated by the Republican Party.

A Pan American Boeing 747 is destroyed by an explosion over the Scottish town of Lockerbie. 259 passengers and crew are killed, plus eleven people on the ground.

The *USS Vincennes* shoots down an Iranian airlines plane over the Persian Gulf. 286 passengers and crew are killed.

Dustin Hoffman and Tom Cruise star in *Rainman*.

Gene Hackman and Willem Dafoe star in *Mississippi Burning*.

Robert Zemeckis's *Who Framed Roger Rabbit?* is released

Thomas Harris publishes *The Silence of the Lambs*.

Stephen Hawking publishes *A Brief History of Time*.

Roseanne appears on U.S. TV.

War and Remembrance appears on U.S. TV.

Curtis Strange becomes the first golfer to earn a million dollars in a season.

Rick Mears wins the Indy 500.

Felix Wankel and Enzo Ferrari die.

1989

Total production approaches 900,000. Six-speed, manual transmission is introduced, along with Selective Ride Control. The Z53 suspension package, with 17-inch wheels and tires becomes standard equipment. A $2000 detachable hardtop for the convertible is made available.

George Bush is sworn in as 41st president of the United States.

The Dow Jones index falls nearly 200 points.

The French celebrate the bicentennial of their revolution.

The Germans celebrate the dismantling of the Berlin Wall.

The Exxon Valdez spills nine million gallons of oil in Prince William Sound, Alaska.

Sony buys Columbia Pictures.

Mitsubishi buys the Rockefeller Center

Panama declares war on the United States.

The United States invades Panama.

Oliver North goes on trail for shredding documents.

Zsa Zsa Gabor goes to jail for slapping a traffic cop.

Michael Keaton stars in *Batman*.

Jessica Tandy stars in *Driving Miss Daisy*.

Lonesome Dove is shown on U.S. TV.

American Greg Lemond wins the Tour de France by the narrowest margin ever.

America qualifies for the soccer world cup for the first time since 1950.

Emperor Hirohito of Japan and Ayatollah Khomeini die.

1990

The ZR1 appears. With near race car specifications, it is the most expensive automobile ever produced by General Motors, retailing at $59,000. The Lotus-developed, all-alloy, four cam, thirty-two valve, 375bhp engine provides a top speed of over 170mph and a 0–60 time of 4.5 seconds.

Nelson Mandela is released after over 25 years imprisonment in South Africa.

Mikhail Gorbachev is awarded the Nobel Prize for Peace.

Iraqi troops invade Kuwait.

U.S. and allied forces engage Iraq in Operation Desert Storm.

Margaret Thatcher resigns as British prime minister and is succeeded by John Major.

Kevin Costner directs and stars in *Dances with Wolves*.

Martin Scorsesi co-scripts and directs *GoodFellas*.

Macauley Culkin stars in *Home Alone*.

Johnny Depp stars in *Edward Scissorhands*.

MC Hammer releases *Please Hammer Don't Hurt 'Em*.

Chris Rea releases *Road to Hell*.

Twin Peaks appears on U.S. TV.

The Simpsons appear on U.S. TV.

Magic Johnson of the LA Lakers is named Most Valuable Player for the third time.

Greg Lemond wins the Tour de France for the third time.

McDonalds open an outlet in Moscow.

Greta Garbo dies.

1991

The Sixth Generation Corvettes, including the *King of the Hill* ZR1 are subtly restyled. To the annoyance of many who had paid over even the astronomic list price of the ZR1, standard 'Vettes got identical rear-end treatment, right down to the squared-off tail lights. To add insult to injury, by mid-year ZR1 prices are being discounted.

Nelson Mandela becomes president of the African National Congress.

Pan Am files for bankruptcy.

The Bank of Credit and Commerce collapses.

U.S. and allied forces expel Iraqi forces from Kuwait.

George Bush and Mikhail Gorbachev agree on a Strategic Arms Reduction Treaty (SALT) to reduce their nuclear weapons stocks by a third.

Sony launches the mini-disc.

Sega Games introduce *Sonic the Hedgehog*.

The first *Planet Hollywood* restaurant opens in New York.

Kevin Costner stars in *JFK*.

Nirvana release *Nevermind*.

Michael Jackson releases *Dangerous*.

Jeff Gordon wins the Daytona 500 in a Chevrolet.

Rick Mears wins the Indy 500 for the fourth time.

The New York Giants beat the Buffalo Bills 20 – 19 in the Super Bowl.

Freddy Mercury and Dr. Seuss die.

1992

Dave Hill takes over as Corvette chief engineer in the middle of a particularly hard time for General Motors, which declares a loss of over seven billion dollars for 1991. The LT-1 version of the 350 small-block is introduced, taking output to 300bhp and performance to within striking distance of the ZR1.

President George Bush vomits and passes out at an official dinner in Japan.

The U.S. fails to sign up to commitments to protect the environment at the Rio Earth Summit.

Mike Tyson is convicted of rape and sent to prison for six years.

Manuel Noriega is convicted of drug trafficking and sent to prison for forty years.

John Gotti is convicted of murder and sent to prison for life.

Prince Charles and Princess Diana separate.

Princess Anne divorces Captain Mark Phillips.

EuroDisney opens near Paris, France.

Madonna publishes *Sex*.

Madonna releases *Erotica*.

Francis Ford Coppola's *Bram Stoker's Dracula* is released.

Spike Lee's *Malcom X* is released.

At the Barcelona Olympics, the U.S.A.'s basketball "Dream Team" take the gold medal.

Briton Nigel Mansell becomes Formula One world champion, having won a record nine Grand Prix in the season.

Marlene Dietrich dies.

1993

The ZR1's awesome power is increased to 405bhp in order to keep it ahead of Dodge's Viper. Top speed now nudges 180mph. All 'Vettes get wider wheels and tires and torque is improved on the LT-1. ZR1 sales are pinned at 448 per year but overall Corvette sales at last improve.

Bill Clinton is sworn in as the 42nd president of the United States.

A bomb explodes at the World Trade Center in New York, killing five people.

The FBI storm the headquarters of the Branch Davidian sect in Waco, Texas. Over 80 people die in the ensuing fire and gun battle.

The Brady Act places controls on the purchase of firearms in the United States.

Snoop Doggy Dog is charged with being an accomplice to murder, and acquitted.

Michael Jackson is charged with child abuse, and acquitted.

Bill Murray stars in *Groundhog Day*.

Sam Neill stars in *Jurassic Park*.

The X-Files appears on U.S. TV.

Frasier appears on U.S. TV.

Bill Clinton has a $200 haircut aboard Air Force One on the runway at Los Angeles.

Evander Holyfield defeats Riddick Bowe to regain the WBA and IBF heavyweight boxing titles.

Nigel Mansell wins the PPG Indycar series at his first attempt.

Frank Zappa and Ferruccio Lamborghini die.

1994

The last LT5 motors are delivered from Mercury Marine. The convertible gains a heated glass rear window. All Corvettes are now fitted with side air bags to comply with federal legislation.

General Motors agrees to fund the government's fifty million dollar vehicle safety research program.

Nelson Mandela is inaugurated as South Africa's first black president.

President Clinton is awarded an honorary degree by Oxford University, England.

Yassir Arafat is awarded the Nobel Prize for Peace.

The Channel Tunnel, linking Britain and France, is opened after seven years' work building it.

F1 driver Ayrton Senna is killed in a crash during the San Merino Grand Prix.

Kurt Cobhain commits suicide.

Johnny Depp stars in *Ed Wood*.

Tom Hanks stars in *Forrest Gump*.

The Rolling Stones release *Voodoo Lounge*.

Beasty Boys release *Ill Communication*.

Boxer George Foreman takes the WBA and IBF world heavyweight titles at age 45.

Golfer Tiger Woods wins the U.S. Amateur Championship at age 18.

Michael Schumacher wins the Formula One world championship.

Oliver McCall winds the WBC world heavyweight boxing title.

John Candy and Telly Savalas die.

1995

527 Pace Car Replicas are produced, of which 415 are for sale. They are equipped with automatic transmission and finished in deep purple over white with a white top and distinctive graphics. All Corvettes get vents in the front fenders, reminiscent of the early Sting Rays.

Rogue trader Nick Leeson manages, single-handedly, to bring down Barings, Britain's oldest merchant bank.

The U.S. dollar is traded at its lowest ever rate on foreign currency markets.

Timothy McVeigh causes an explosion at a Federal Building in Oklahoma City, killing 166 people.

Members of the Solar Temple sect commit group suicide in Quebec, Canada, and Grenoble, Switzerland.

The U.S. Space Shuttle Atlantis dock with the Russian Space Station Mir.

Alan Hale and Thomas Bopp discover the Hale-Bopp comet.

Waterworld is released.

Pocahantas is released.

Michael Jackson releases *HIStory*.

Pearl Jam release *Mirrorball*.

Basketball player Michael Jordan comes out of retirement to rejoin the Chicago Bulls.

Jacques Villeneuve wins the Indy 500.

The Harlem Globetrotters lose their first game in 24 years, after 8,829 wins in a row.

Juan Manuel Fangio dies.

1996

A 330bhp LT4 version of the small block V8 is produced, running a compression ration of 10.8:1. It is only available with manual transmission. A limited edition of 1000 "Grand Sports" are produced, fitted with the LT4 and finished in Admiral Blue with a white stripe. A Sebring Silver Collectors Edition is also produced.

General Motors introduce the world's first volume-production electric automobile, the Saturn EV1. It has a top speed in excess of 80mph and can accelerate to 60mph in 8.5 seconds.

The Taliban, an extreme, Muslim-fundamentalist group, become the effective governors of Afghanistan.

Bill Clinton is re-elected president of the United States.

Madeleine Albright becomes first female U.S. Secretary of State.

Independence Day is released.

Mission Impossible is released.

Ralph Fiennes stars in *The English Patient*.

Sheryl Crow releases *Sheryl Crow*.

The 26th Olympic Games take place in Atlanta, Georgia: the United States wins 44 gold medals.

Mike Tyson regains the WBC world heavyweight title from Frank Bruno

Evander Holyfield regains the WBA world heavyweight title from Mike Tyson.

Tiger Woods becomes the first golfer to win the U.S. amateur championship three times in succession.

Damon Hill wins the Formula One world championship.

George Burns dies.

1997

The Seventh Generation Corvette debuts. It is all new, the most comfortable and fuel-efficient ever, with an all new engine: the all-aluminum LS1. The new car is lighter and more powerful that its predecessor and is received with great enthusiasm by Press and pubic alike.

The Dow Jones index records its biggest fall ever: 554 points. Trading is suspended.

O. J. Simpson is convicted of causing the death of his wife and a friend.

Hong Kong returns to Chinese government after over a hundred and fifty years of British administration.

Princess Diana and Dodi Fayed are killed in an automobile crash in Paris, along with their driver, Henri Paul.

Thirty-nine members of the Heaven's Gate sect commit suicide in California.

Ang Lee's *The Ice Storm* is released.

James Cameron's *Titanic* is released.

Bjork releases *Homogenic*.

Elton John releases *Candle in the Wind '97*.

Michael Flatley opens *Lord of the Dance*.

21 year-old Tiger Woods becomes the youngest-ever winner of the U.S. Masters golf tournament.

Jacques Villeneuve wins the Formula One world championship.

Mike Tyson is disqualified from a WBA title fight for biting off part of Evander Holyfield's ear.

Mother Theresa dies.

1998

A sensational new convertible is introduced. The Corvette is once more selected as the Indianapolis Pace Car and a special replica is produced—in special, Pace Car Purple with yellow wheels and graphics and a black and yellow, leather interior. The convertible features a separate trunk for the first time since 1962.

The U.S. budget balances for the first time in thirty years.

The Chrysler Corporation merges with Daimler-Benz to become Daimler-Chrysler.

President Clinton is accused of improper behaviour with White House intern Monica Lewinsky.

Britain bans the possession of hand guns.

An abortion clinic in Birmingham, Alabama, is bombed.

Theodore Kacynski—the "Unabomber"—is sentenced to four life terms plus thirty years.

The remains of the last Tsar of Russia and his family are reburied in St. Petersburg.

Thirteen factory workers in Ohio win the world's biggest ever lottery payout: $161,000,000.

Tom Hanks stars in *Saving Private Ryan*.

Mike Myers stars in *Austin Powers: International Man of Mystery*.

Jerry Seinfeld stops starring in *Seinfeld*.

Eddie Cheever wins the Indy 500.

Mika Hakkinen wins the Formula One world championship.

Marco Pantani wins the Tour de France—and the Giro d'Italia.

Tammy Wynette and Roy Rogers die.

1999

A hardtop Corvette is introduced as an entry-level model. Six-speed, manual transmission and the Z51 suspension came as standard though interior trim was limited to black. '99 options included a fighter-plane-like Head-Up Display system and Twilight Sentinel.

In Kosovo, NATO forces begin Operation Allied Force.

Nelson Mandela steps down as president of South Africa.

Tobacco companies admit to harm caused by cigarette smoking

Movie Star Carmen Electra files for divorce from LA Lakers Star Dennis Rodman.

Basketball legend Michael Jordan retires for the second time.

Jeff Gordon wins the Daytona 500.

World motorcycle champion Michael Doohan is injured in the Spanish Grand Prix.

Tiger Woods wins the PGA championship.

Michael Schumacher wins the Formula One world championship.

Lance Armstrong wins the Tour de France

The Matrix is released.

Star Wars Episode 1—The Phantom Menace is released.

Blair Witch Project is released.

Rage Against The Machine release *The Battle of Los Angeles*.

Red Hot Chili Peppers release *Californication*.

Monica Lewinsky publishes a book, *Monica's Story*, written with Andrew Morton, telling her side of her affair with Bill Clinton.

Victor Mature and George C. Scott die.

2000

A special Millennium Edition is produced, in striking, Millennium Yellow. This recalls the C5R racing Corvettes that were enjoying increasing success in endurance racing at Seb ring, Daytona and in the Le Mans 24-Hour race. The wheel spokes are slimmed down and interior trim is revised and improved.

Smith & Wesson limit the manufacture and distribution of hand guns.

South Carolina removes the Confederate flag from the Capitol Dome.

The "I love you" virus causes worldwide disruption to computer systems.

Dale Jarrett wins the Daytona 500.

Venus Williams wins the Wimbledon and U.S. open championships and a Gold medal at the Sydney Olympic Games.

Tiger Woods wins the PGA championship.

Michael Schumacher wins the Formula One world championship.

Lance Armstrong wins the Tour de France.

Gladiator is released.

Cast Away is released.

Scary Movie is released.

The Beatles release "1"

U2 release *All That You Can't Leave Behind*.

Madonna releases *Music*.

Charles Schultz and Patrick O'Brian die.

Hedy Lamarr dies

2001

The Z06 is introduced as a replacement for the Hardtop. The new LS6 engine is rated at 385bhp – more powerful than the first generation ZR1s. The Z06 has practical vents for rear brake cooling, red-colored brake calipers and signature wheels fitted with run-flat Goodyear Eagle Supercar tires.

George W. Bush is sworn in as 43rd. president of the United States.

Terrorists fly two airliners into the twin towers of the World Trade Center in New York and into the Pentagon in Washington DC. A fourth plane comes down outside Pittsburgh.

The Taliban regime in Afghanistan collapses after a sustained attack by U.S. and allied forces.

Harlem Globetrotters Meadowlark Lemon (#36) and Marques Haynes (#20) join Wilt Chamberlain (#13) in the distinction of having their numbers retired by the team.

Dale Earnhardt is killed on the last lap of the Daytona 500. Michael Waltrip wins.

Dale Earnhardt Jnr. crashes on the first lap of the DuraLube 400 but is uninjured.

Michael Schumacher wins the Formula One world championship.

Lance Armstrong wins the Tour de France.

Harry Potter and The Sorcerer's Stone is released.

The Lord of the Rings—The Fellowship of the Ring is released.

Bob Dylan releases *Love and Theft*.

Alicia Keys releases *Songs in A Minor*.

Anthony Quinn dies.

Larry Adler dies

2002

Z06 output is increased to a staggering 405bhp, making it by far the most powerful 350 ever. All Corvettes now coast over $40,000. The Corvette is chosen to pace the Indy 500 for the fifth time. Three Pace Car Replicas are produced, but they are not for sale.

The U.S. incarcerates prisoners of war from the campaign in Afghanistan in Guantanamo Bay, Cuba.

U.S. reporter Daniel Pearl is murdered in Pakistan.

The U.S. Justice Department opens a criminal investigation into collapsed energy company Enron Corp.

Horror writer Stephen King announces his retirement.

Queen Elizabeth II of England celebrates her Golden Jubilee.

Queen Elizabeth, the Queen Mother, dies aged 101.

WorldCom files for bankruptcy.

Ward Burton wins the Daytona 500.

Sprinter Tim Montgomery becomes the fastest man on earth, covering 100 meters in 9.78 seconds.

Martin Buser wins the Iditarod Sled Dog Race for the fourth time.

Lance Armstrong wins the Tour de France for the fourth time.

Star Wars II – The Attack of the Clones in released.

The Lord of the Rings – The Two Towers is released.

Blind Boys of Alabama release *Higher Ground*.

Bruce Springsteen and the E Street Band release *The Rising*.

Billy Wilder and James Coburn die.

Linda Lovelace, porn star, and Ann Landers, agony aunt, die.

2003

The Corvette is fifty. The Anniversary model is available in a special 50th Red with Champagne tinted wheels and two tone Shale interior. The new F55 Selective Magnetic Ride control is fitted to all Anniversary models. This system allows the cars ride to be monitored and adjusted every half an inch traveled at sixty miles per hour.